GENE MALIS

THE GREAT MOVIE QUIZ

BARNES & NOBLE BOOKS
A DIVISION OF HARPER & ROW, PUBLISHERS
New York, Cambridge, Hagerstown, Philadelphia,
San Francisco, London, Mexico City, São Paulo, Sydney

FIRST EDITION

Designed by Trish Parcell

Library of Congress Cataloging in Publication Data

Malis, Gene.
  The great movie quiz book.

  1. Moving-pictures—Miscellanea. I. Title.
PN1993.85.M34   791.43   80–7760
ISBN 0–06–463518–X (pbk.)

80 81 82 83 84 10 9 8 7 6 5 4 3 2 1

Contents

*A photo section follows pages
36 and 129*

Introduction

The Great Movie Quiz challenges you to recall some of your most exciting and entertaining moments spent in the magic darkness of the movie theater.

You will be amazed at how many movies and specific scenes you can recall vividly! As you tackle the questions, that marvelous camera in your mind will replay those "bigger than life" moments you have watched on the big screen.

You and your friends will find that *The Great Movie Quiz* is a uniquely enjoyable challenge that will unlock for you a treasure house of great memories.

HOW TO SCORE YOURSELF: The Quiz consists of questions on ten different film categories (listed on the Contents page). Each category consists of 100 questions worth one point each. Therefore you can score up to 100 points in each film category.

Within each category there are four types of questions:

1. **Name that star!** Each question briefly describes the star and lists some of his or her film credits.
2. **Name that star! multiple choice** Each question gives five choices from which you must select the correct answer.
3. **Name that movie!** You are given a brief synopsis of the movie and a list of the key members of its cast.
4. **True or False?** A statement is made about a movie or a star and you must decide if it is true or false.

Here's a guide for rating your scores in any particular film category:

85 points or higher	Great!
75–84 points.	Excellent!
60–74 points.	Good
40–59 points.	Fair
Under 40 points	Better pay more attention to the Late Late Show

A TIP ON WORKING THIS QUIZ: Start by selecting the film category that you are most knowledgable about and then go on to the more difficult film categories.

CONTESTS: A great idea is to share *The Great Movie Quiz* with others. You can organize a "movie quiz game." Set up opposing teams and give each team a piece of paper on which they can record their answers. Read each question aloud and allow 30 seconds for each team to give their answers. When each section of a particular quiz is completed (Name that star!, Name that movie!, etc.), check the answers in the back of this book and record the contestants' scores. Then move on to the next type of quiz question. Finally, add up the total scores for each film category and announce the winner(s)!

Adventure-
Suspense-
Thrillers

This major film category is quite broad. It includes any "adventure-suspense-thriller" type of film that cannot be classified in any of our other categories (western, gangster-detective, war, etc.). The films we're going to cover are soldier-of-fortune adventures, murder mysteries, spy intrigues, swashbucklers, etc. They are the kinds of films that are packed with action, drama, excitement and tension. You will surely be reminded of some of your favorite edge-of-the-seat movie-going experiences as you work your way through the next 100 quiz questions.

Name that star!

1. This lanky, top Hollywood star appeared in as many Hitch-cock thrillers* as anyone else.

FILM CREDITS: Call Northside 777 *(1947)*
    *Rope *(1948)*
    *Rear Window *(1954)*
    *The Man Who Knew Too Much *(1956)*
    *Vertigo *(1958)*
    Anatomy of a Murder *(1959)*

Name that star!

2. Basically a romantic comedy star, this suave fellow also appeared in several adventure films along with a few Hitchcock thrillers*.

FILM CREDITS: Gunga Din *(1939)*
    *Notorious *(1946)*
    *To Catch a Thief *(1955)*
    The Pride and the Passion *(1957)*
    *North by Northwest *(1959)*
    Charade *(1964)*

Name that star!

3. One of Hollywood's superstars of the forties and fifties, he leapt to stardom as a swashbuckling hero.

FILM CREDITS: Captain Blood *(1935)*
    The Charge of the Light Brigade *(1936)*
    The Sea Hawk *(1940)*
    Kim *(1951)*
    Mara Maru *(1952)*
    Against All Flags *(1952)*

Name that star!

4. This tall, quiet Hollywood legend made a number of memorable adventure films.

FILM CREDITS: Lives of a Bengal Lancer *(1935)*
Souls at Sea *(1937)*
The Adventures of Marco Polo *(1938)*
Beau Geste *(1939)*
Northwest Mounted Police *(1940)*
For Whom the Bell Tolls *(1943)*

Name that star!

5. A popular leading man of the thirties, he went on to become a good actor working in a variety of films. He won an Academy Award for his role in *Lost Weekend.*

FILM CREDITS: Beau Geste *(1939)*
The Uninvited *(1944)*
Ministry of Fear *(1944)*
The Lost Weekend *(1945)*
Golden Earrings *(1947)*
The Big Clock *(1948)*
Dial M for Murder *(1954)*

Name that star!

6. Another Hollywood superstar of the thirties and forties, he played romantic adventure roles with great success.

FILM CREDITS: Suez *(1938)*
The Rains Came *(1939)*
The Mark of Zorro *(1940)*
Blood and Sand *(1941)*
The Black Swan *(1942)*
Captain from Castile *(1947)*

Name that star!

7. This mild-mannered leading man, with the air of a Southern country gentleman, always turned in a professional performance.

FILM CREDITS: Journey into Fear *(1942)*
Shadow of a Doubt *(1943)*
Portrait of Jennie *(1948)*
The Third Man *(1949)*
Blueprint for Murder *(1953)*
Hush . . . Hush, Sweet Charlotte *(1964)*

Name that star!

8. One of filmland's top romantic leading men, he seems equally effective in suspense and action films.

FILM CREDITS: Spellbound *(1945)*
The Macomber Affair *(1947)*
The Paradine Case *(1947)*
Captain Horatio Hornblower *(1951)*
Moby Dick *(1956)*
Arabesque *(1966)*

Name that star!

9. This attractive redhead always managed to play a gutsy spitfire type.

FILM CREDITS: Beau Geste *(1939)*
Reap the Wild Wind *(1942)*
Jack London *(1943)*
Deadline at Dawn *(1946)*
They Won't Believe Me *(1947)*
I Want to Live *(1958)*

Name that star!

10. She was one of Hollywood's glamour queens in the forties and fifties, not a great actress, but a "type."

FILM CREDITS: The Lady in Question *(1940)*
Blood and Sand *(1941)*
Gilda *(1946)*
They Came to Cordura *(1959)*
The Wrath of God *(1972)*

Name that star!

11. She is a beautiful redhead, a very pleasant and perhaps underrated actress.

FILM CREDITS: The Hunchback of Notre Dame *(1939)*
The Black Swan *(1942)*
The Fallen Sparrow *(1943)*
Sinbad the Sailor *(1947)*
Lady Godiva *(1955)*
Our Man in Havana *(1959)*

Name that star!

12. A top Hollywood actress, she always played outspoken women capable of standing on their own.

FILM CREDITS: Double Indemnity *(1944)*
The Strange Love of Martha Ivers *(1946)*
The Two Mrs. Carrolls *(1947)*
Sorry, Wrong Number *(1948)*
Clash by Night *(1952)*
Titanic *(1953)*

Name that star!

13. A pretty brunette, she has played many just-another-pretty-face roles while top stardom has eluded her.

FILM CREDITS: Scaramouche *(1952)*
Houdini *(1953)*
Prince Valiant *(1954)*
Safari *(1956)*
The Vikings *(1958)*
Psycho *(1960)*

Name that star!

14. A tough-guy type, he played many action roles, but demonstrated his dramatic abilities whenever the opportunity presented itself. He won an Academy Award for *Elmer Gantry.*

FILM CREDITS: His Majesty O'Keefe *(1954)*
Trapeze *(1956)*
Elmer Gantry *(1960)*
The Gypsy Moths *(1969)*
Airport *(1969)*
Scorpio *(1973)*

Name that star!

15. A major star in the forties and fifties, he was soft-spoken, smooth and sinister. He always played a soldier of fortune involved in danger.

FILM CREDITS: China *(1946)*
Two Years Before the Mast *(1946)*
Calcutta *(1947)*
Appointment with Danger *(1951)*
Botany Bay *(1953)*
Boy on a Dolphin *(1957)*

Name that star!

16. He was a handsome romantic screen idol who ranked right alongside Gable, Power and Flynn.

FILM CREDITS: High Wall *(1947)*
The Bribe *(1949)*
Valley of the Kings *(1954)*
The House of the Seven Hawks *(1959)*
Killers of Kilimanjaro *(1960)*
The Night Walker *(1964)*

Name that star!

17. A Hollywood legend in his own time, he was a much finer actor than many realized.

FILM CREDITS: Mutiny on the Bounty *(1935)*
Call of the Wild *(1935)*
Test Pilot *(1938)*
Strange Cargo *(1940)*
Boom town *(1940)*
Mogambo *(1954)*

Name that star!

18. He could play the role of a swashbuckling hero in his sleep. No one else ever played that kind of role with comparable zest.

FILM CREDITS: The Dawn Patrol *(1930)*
The Prisoner of Zenda *(1937)*
Gunga Din *(1939)*
Safari *(1940)*
The Corsican Brothers *(1941)*
Sinbad the Sailor *(1947)*

Name that star!

19. A major star since the fifties, this robust leading man always plays dynamic roles.

FILM CREDITS: Ace in the Hole *(1951)*
The Big Trees *(1952)*
Twenty Thousand Leagues Under the Sea *(1954)*
The List of Adrian Messenger *(1963)*
Seven Days in May *(1964)*
The Light at the Edge of the World *(1971)*

Name that star!

20. He is noted for playing "heroic" heroes with unrivaled grandeur.

FILM CREDITS: The Naked Jungle *(1954)*
Touch of Evil *(1958)*
The Buccaneer *(1958)*
The Wreck of the Mary Deare *(1959)*
Khartoum *(1966)*
Skyjacked *(1972)*

Name that star!

Name that star!

Multiple choice

1. *The Sea Wolf* (1941), a film based upon the famous Jack London novel, starred _____?
a. Edward G. Robinson **b.** Errol Flynn **c.** Robert Ryan
d. Clark Gable **e.** Alan Ladd

2. Who starred in that famous Hitchcock thriller *Psycho* (1960)?
a. Gregory Peck **b.** Richard Widmark **c.** Anthony Perkins
d. Lee Marvin **e.** Peter Lorre

3. Who starred with Dean Martin in *Airport* (1969)?
a. Charlton Heston **b.** William Holden **c.** Karl Malden
d. Burt Lancaster **e.** Kirk Douglas

4. In the 1944 remake of *Gaslight,* a superb suspense film, who starred with Ingrid Bergman and Joseph Cotten?
a. Charles Boyer **b.** Tyrone Power **c.** Paul Henreid
d. Walter Pidgeon **e.** Gary Cooper

5. In that classic swashbuckler, *The Count of Monte Cristo* (1934), who starred as Edmond Dantes?
a. Errol Flynn **b.** Robert Donat **c.** Douglas Fairbanks, Jr.
d. Tyrone Power **e.** Rex Harrison

6. *Anatomy of a Murder* (1959) starred which of these well-known actresses?
a. Lee Remick **b.** Carroll Baker **c.** Susan Hayward
d. Ida Lupino **e.** Kim Novak

7. Who starred in *The Lady Vanishes* (1934), one of Hitchcock's excellent thrillers?
a. John Mills **b.** Alec Guinness **c.** Dirk Bogarde
d. Richard Burton **e.** Michael Redgrave

8. Otto Preminger directed a memorable thriller, *Bunny Lake Is Missing* (1965). Who starred?
a. Laurence Harvey   **b.** Laurence Olivier   **c.** James Mason
d. Robert Mitchum   **e.** Joseph Cotten

9. Who had top billing in the star-packed adventure film *Around the World in Eighty Days* (1956)?
a. James Mason   **b.** Gregory Peck   **c.** Alec Guinness
d. Peter O'Toole   **e.** David Niven

10. When the famous Dickens novel *Oliver Twist* was made into a movie in 1948, who starred as Fagin?
a. Robert Newton   **b.** Charles Laughton   **c.** Alec Guinness
d. Ronald Colman   **e.** Douglas Fairbanks, Jr.

11. Who starred in that swashbuckler *Scaramouche* (1952)?
a. Stewart Granger   **b.** Errol Flynn   **c.** Tyrone Power
d. David Niven   **e.** George Sanders

12. Life in a mental institution had everyone on the edge of their seats in *The Snake Pit* (1948). Who was the star of this thriller?
a. Olivia De Havilland   **b.** Joan Fontaine   **c.** Bette Davis
d. Barbara Stanwyck   **e.** Ida Lupino

13. *Portrait of Jennie* (1948) was a strange story about an artist and his portrait of a girl. Who played the role of Jennie?
a. Gene Tierney   **b.** Jennifer Jones   **c.** Sophia Loren
d. Loretta Young   **e.** Vivien Leigh

14. *The Spiral Staircase* (1946) was a certified, old-house-in-a-thunderstorm thriller. Who starred?
a. Dorothy McGuire   **b.** Anne Baxter   **c.** Joan Crawford
d. Joan Fontaine   **e.** Bette Davis

15. A hard-bitten government agent goes on a worldwide hunt for a narcotics gang in *To the Ends of the Earth* (1948).

Who starred with Signe Hasso in this thriller?
a. Humphrey Bogart **b.** Alan Ladd **c.** Dick Powell
d. Lloyd Nolan **e.** John Garfield

16. Who played the female lead in *Spellbound* (1945)?
a. Gene Tierney **b.** Joan Fontaine **c.** Jennifer Jones
d. Ingrid Bergman **e.** Alexis Smith

17. Who starred with Sean Connery in the first James Bond
superadventure film *Dr. No* (1962)?
a. Honor Blackman **b.** Jill St. John **c.** Ursula Andress
d. Janice Rule **e.** Janet Leigh

18. One of Hitchcock's masterpieces of suspense, *Strangers
on a Train* (1951), starred Farley Granger and _____?
a. Robert Walker **b.** Dan Duryea **c.** Edmond O'Brien
d. James Stewart **e.** Glenn Ford

19. Cedric Hardwicke played Livingstone in *Stanley and Livingstone* (1939). Who played Stanley?
a. Clark Gable **b.** Spencer Tracy **c.** Fredric March
d. Robert Young **e.** Ronald Colman

20. Who starred with Robert Redford in *Three Days of the
Condor* (1975)?
a. Lee Remick **b.** Karen Black **c.** Sophia Loren
d. Faye Dunaway **e.** Carroll Baker

21. *Crisis* (1950) is the story of a brain surgeon who is forced
to operate on a South American dictator while his wife is a
captive of revolutionaries. Who starred in this thriller?
a. Gregory Peck **b.** Cary Grant **c.** William Holden
d. Walter Pidgeon **e.** Ronald Reagan

22. *The Crowded Sky* (1960) tells the tale of two planes
flying toward each other on a collision course. Who starred
with Rhonda Fleming and Efrem Zimbalist, Jr. in this thriller?

a. Dana Andrews **b.** Edmond O'Brien **c.** Robert Stack
d. Richard Widmark **e.** Richard Egan

23. *Cry Terror* (1958), the story of an airplane bomber, starred Rod Steiger, Inger Stevens and a well-known British actor. What was his name?
a. Michael Redgrave **b.** James Mason **c.** Alec Guinness
d. Ralph Richardson **e.** Trevor Howard

24. The spy thriller *A Dandy in Aspic* (1968) tells the bizarre tale of a double agent in Berlin who receives orders to kill himself. Who starred?
a. Michael Caine **b.** James Coburn **c.** Laurence Harvey
d. Robert Mitchum **e.** Joseph Cotten

25. In *Dangerous Crossing* (1953) a woman's husband disappears and she can't prove he ever existed; meanwhile he is trying to kill her. Who starred with Jeanne Crain in this tense tale?
a. Ralph Bellamy **b.** Rex Harrison **c.** Michael Rennie
d. Preston Foster **e.** Stewart Granger

26. Who starred in the spy thriller *Funeral in Berlin* (1967)?
a. Peter O'Toole **b.** Michael Caine **c.** George Segal
d. Robert Shaw **e.** Peter Lawford

27. A military takeover of the American government is attempted in *Seven Days in May* (1964). Who starred in the role of the President?
a. George Sanders **b.** George C. Scott **c.** Henry Fonda
d. Frederic March **e.** Gregory Peck

28. Who starred with James Stewart in the 1956 remake of *The Man Who Knew Too Much?*
a. Rita Hayworth **b.** Deborah Kerr **c.** Doris Day
d. Carroll Baker **e.** Katharine Hepburn

29. *Scorpio* (1972) is a story about dirty work inside the CIA. Who starred with Burt Lancaster in this thriller?
a. Michael Caine   **b.** James Coburn   **c.** Alain Delon
d. Albert Finney   **e.** George Kennedy

30. Who starred as the British secret-service man in *The Quiller Memorandum* (1966)?
a. George Segal   **b.** Richard Burton   **c.** Rex Harrison
d. James Mason   **e.** Trevor Howard

31. In *Blindfold* (1965), who starred opposite Claudia Cardinale as the psychiatrist enlisted by the CIA for a special job?
a. Gregory Peck   **b.** William Holden   **c.** Charlton Heston
d. Rock Hudson   **e.** Glenn Ford

32. *An Experiment in Terror* (1962) starred Lee Remick. Who co-starred?
a. Richard Conte   **b.** Frank Sinatra   **c.** Richard Widmark
d. Robert Ryan   **e.** Glenn Ford

33. *The Woman in the Window* (1944) starred Edward G. Robinson as a mild-mannered professor who meets a girl who involves him in a murder. Who played that girl?
a. Susan Hayward   **b.** Jane Greer   **c.** Joan Bennett
d. Loretta Young   **e.** Ann Sheridan

34. *Dark Passage* (1947) tells the story of a convicted murderer who escapes from jail to prove his innocence. Who co-starred with Humphrey Bogart in this exciting film?
a. Lauren Bacall   **b.** Gloria Grahame   **c.** Lizabeth Scott
d. Veronica Lake   **e.** Priscilla Lane

35. A high-tension thriller, *Out of the Past* (1947), starred Robert Mitchum as a private eye and Kirk Douglas as a hood who hires him to find his girlfriend. Who played the girl?
a. Rita Hayworth   **b.** Jane Greer   **c.** Susan Hayward
d. Virginia Mayo   **e.** Alexis Smith

36. Who played the psychiatrist in *The President's Analyst* (1967)?
a. Steve McQueen **b.** Gig Young **c.** Rod Steiger
d. James Coburn **e.** Peter Lawford

37. Who starred in *Grand Prix* (1966), a story about daredevil race drivers?
a. Steve McQueen **b.** James Garner **c.** Clint Eastwood
d. Paul Newman **e.** Kirk Douglas

38. Who played the title role in *The Lady from Shanghai* (1948)?
a. Ida Lupino **b.** Hedy Lamarr **c.** Vivien Leigh **d.** Marlene Dietrich **e.** Rita Hayworth

39. A mad bomber threatens an ocean liner in *Juggernaut* (1974). Who starred?
a. Richard Harris **b.** Robert Shaw **c.** Richard Burton
d. Charles Bronson **e.** Burt Lancaster

40. *The High and the Mighty* (1954)—probably the inspiration for the *Airport* films—starred _____?
a. Robert Taylor **b.** John Wayne **c.** Clark Gable
d. Robert Young **e.** James Stewart

Name that movie!

1. An Air Force bomber carrying an atomic bomb is accidentally sent out to destroy Moscow. The plane cannot be stopped, and so the President orders the destruction of New York City to pacify the Russians and avert an atomic war. A tense black adventure-comedy that is particularly chilling because something like it could happen to us any day.

THE CAST: Henry Fonda, Walter Matthau, Dan O'Herlihy, Frank Overton, Fritz Weaver, Edward Binns, Larry Hagman

Name that movie!

2. A brainwashed Korean veteran returns home. He has been programmed to kill a prominent politician, and the person who can trigger him to carry out his mission is his own mother. A terrific spy thriller that grabs you and doesn't let go for a minute.

THE CAST: Frank Sinatra, Laurence Harvey, Janet Leigh, James Gregory, Angela Lansbury, Henry Silva, John McGiver

Name that movie!

3. A news photographer sitting home with a broken leg witnesses a murder in an apartment across his courtyard. Hitchcock and a fine cast make this a memorable thriller.

THE CAST: James Stewart, Grace Kelly, Raymond Burr, Judith Evelyn, Wendell Corey, Thelma Ritter

Name that movie!

4. This remake of *Outward Bound* (that's not the title this time) tells the weird story of a group of people who find themselves aboard a luxury liner, without knowing how they got there. Gradually, they come to the realization that they are all dead and bound for the next world. An intriguing plot that haunts you after you've left the theater.

THE CAST: John Garfield, Edmund Gwenn, Eleanor Parker, Paul Henreid, Sydney Greenstreet, Faye Emerson

Name that movie!

5. This adventure story by Kipling tells the tale of two soldiers of fortune in India in the 1880s. They contact a remote tribe who accepts them as kings, but greed is their undoing.

THE CAST: Sean Connery, Michael Caine, Christopher Plummer

Name that movie!

6. A marvelous adventure story about a band of rebels and rogues who live in the forest and battle the local oppressive authorities in merry old England. Hits the bull's-eye as one of the finest action-adventure films ever made!

THE CAST: Errol Flynn, Olivia De Havilland, Basil Rathbone, Claude Rains, Eugene Pallette, Alan Hale, Patric Knowles, Melville Cooper, Una O'Connor, Ian Hunter

Name that movie!

7. In this British-made film, a science professor engaged in atomic research threatens to blow up London with a bomb, within a specified time period, unless the government halts his research project. A solid suspense story that hits a nerve very close to home.

THE CAST: Barry Jones, Olive Sloane, André Morell, Joan Hickson

Name that movie!

8. An over-the-hill boxer discovers that he still has the pride and guts to stand up against gangsters who order him to throw his last fight. A gem of a low-budget film that is moving and charged with suspense.

THE CAST: Robert Ryan, Audrey Totter, George Tobias, Alan Baxter, Wallace Ford

Name that movie!

9. A growing element of suspense and suspicion creeps into the life of a family in a small town when an uncle comes to visit. As it turns out, the police are after him as the Merry Widow Murderer. The master of suspense, aided by a fine cast, scores again!

THE CAST: Joseph Cotten, Teresa Wright, Hume Cronyn, MacDonald Carey

Name that movie!

10. Seven Germans escape from a concentration camp and the Nazis hunt them down; one escapes. A gripping story, with a talented cast playing it to the hilt.

THE CAST: Spencer Tracy, Signe Hasso, Hume Cronyn, Jessica Tandy, Agnes Moorehead, Felix Bressart, George Macready, George Zucco

Name that movie!

11. Sinbad the Sailor hunts for the legendary roc's egg which will restore his midget fiancée to her normal size. (There's been some dirty work done here by a nasty magician.) A marvelous fantasy adventure with excellent special effects.

THE CAST: Kerwin Mathews, Kathryn Grant (Crosby), Torin Thatcher, Richard Eyer, Alec Mango

Name that movie!

12. This fast-paced adventure film, based on a famous novel by Henry Fielding, is set in eighteenth-century England. A foundling boy has many wild experiences in the process of growing up and finally marries the daughter of the man who took him in and reared him. A panorama of bawdy adventures done in an innovative style that is refreshingly entertaining.

THE CAST: Albert Finney, Susannah York, Hugh Griffith, Edith Evans, Joan Greenwood, Diane Cilento

Name that movie!

13. An artist with severe mental problems paints pictures of his succeeding wives depicting them as the Angel of Death. Then, he murders them by giving them a glass of poisoned milk. A cast of real pros manages to create a gripping thriller out of this one, despite a limp plot.

THE CAST: Barbara Stanwyck, Humphrey Bogart, Alexis Smith, Nigel Bruce

Name that movie!

14. A British secret agent foils an arch criminal who tries to destroy Fort Knox in order to make his personal hoard of gold more valuable on the world market. A thoroughly enjoyable adventure film, fast-paced and studded with spectacular action sequences.

THE CAST: Sean Connery, Honor Blackman, Gert Frobe, Harold Sakata, Shirley Eaton, Bernard Lee, Lois Maxwell

Name that movie!

15. This grim but gripping movie tells the story of the secret leader of the IRA and how he becomes so involved in committing acts of violence and terror that he loses sight of his cause.

It makes a point worth noting: namely, that a revolution is only as worthwhile as the true motives of the revolutionaries.

THE CAST: James Cagney, Glynis Johns, Don Murray, Dana Wynter, Michael Redgrave, Sybil Thorndike, Cyril Cusack, Niall MacGinnis, Richard Harris

Name that movie!

16. A World War II veteran returns home to find that his unfaithful wife has been murdered and that he is suspected of the crime. A crackerjack mystery thriller, with a cast that plays this kind of thing the way Olivier plays *Hamlet*!

THE CAST: Alan Ladd, Veronica Lake, William Bendix, Howard da Silva, Doris Dowling, Tom Powers, Hugh Beaumont

Name that movie!

17. A famous pirate named Morgan is made the governor of the island of Jamaica. His job is to rid the Caribbean of all buccaneers, and he rounds up his old cronies to do the job. A big, swashbuckling action yarn in high gear! They don't know how to make them like this any more.

THE CAST: Tyrone Power, Maureen O'Hara, Laird Cregar, Thomas Mitchell, George Sanders, Anthony Quinn, George Zucco

Name that movie!

18. In this funny crime caper four crooks cleverly plan to rob the Brooklyn Museum of a priceless diamond. A refreshing winner!

THE CAST: Robert Redford, George Segal, Zero Mostel, Paul Sand, Ron Leibman, Moses Gunn, William Redfield

Name that movie!

.19. Four people attempt to escape a revolution in India, but their plane crashes in the Tibetan mountains. They are found by some strange mountain natives who take them to a hidden valley where a Utopian civilization exists. The story is based on a famous novel by James Hilton. The film is a classic adventure fantasy!

THE CAST: Ronald Colman, H. B. Warner, Thomas Mitchell, Edward Everett Horton, Isabel Jewell, Jane Wyatt, Margo, John Howard, Sam Jaffe

Name that movie!

20. A new doctor takes over as the head of a mental institution. But he turns out to be an impostor who is suffering from amnesia. A female member of the staff falls in love with him and helps him recall what happened to the real doctor whom he is impersonating. Hitchcock turns out another classic!

THE CAST: Ingrid Bergman, Gregory Peck, Leo. G. Carroll, Michael Chekhov, Rhonda Fleming, John Emery

Name that movie!

True or false?

1. Cornel Wilde played a naked man running for his life through the wilds of Africa in *The Naked Prey* (1966).

2. *The Spy Who Came in from the Cold* (1966) starred Burt Lancaster.

3. Charlton Heston starred in *Airport* (1969).

4. *Enter the Dragon* (1973) starred Bruce Lee.

5. *Odd Man Out* (1946) was a psychological drama.

6. The actor who played the captain of the ship in *The Poseidon Adventure* (1972) was Leslie Nielsen.

7. The role of the shark hunter in *Jaws* (1975) was played by Robert Shaw.

8. In *The Ipcress File* (1965), secret agent Harry Palmer was played by Michael Caine.

9. The title role in *Gunga Din* (1939) was played by Sam Jaffe.

10. Alan Ladd starred in the 1941 screen version of Jack London's adventure story *The Sea Wolf*.

11. George Maharis starred as the special government agent investigating the disappearance of a virus called *The Satan Bug* (1965).

12. *Casino Royale* (1967), a James Bond adventure film, starred David Niven as James Bond.

13. *The Mackintosh Man* (1973) starred Paul Newman as a government agent.

14. *The Candidate* (1972) was a drama about politics starring Robert Redford.

15. In *Captain Nemo and the Underwater City* (1969), James Mason played the role of Nemo.

16. Gregory Peck co-starred with Orson Welles in the classic *Citizen Kane* (1941).

17. *The Picture of Dorian Gray* (1945) starred Hurd Hatfield as Dorian Gray.

18. Tony Curtis played the lead in *Prince Valiant* (1954), an adventure film based on a famous comic strip.

19. Lorne Greene (of *Bonanza* fame) played Ava Gardner's father in *Earthquake* (1974).

20. In *From Russia with Love* (1963), Robert Shaw plays a Russian spy who tries to kill James Bond.

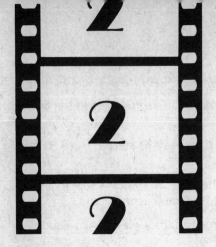

Musicals

Now, let's go back to the most joyful movie memories of all—
the musicals. Remember all those great tunes and terrific
dance production numbers, the beautiful costumes and those
lavish sets!

"Words and music" was the movie-making formula in Hollywood that resulted in so many brilliant musicals throughout
the thirties, forties and fifties. The list of top musical stars
is just too long to enumerate here. It includes such unforgettable greats as Astaire, Rogers, Garland, Grayson, Grable, Faye,
Rooney, Kelly, O'Connor, Sinatra, Day and Keel. Then, sadly,
due to rising production costs and a trend toward "realism,"

the production of big musical films ceased. For the past fifteen years or so there have been only occasional film versions of successful Broadway musicals.

Today, the only way to see some of the great musicals of the past is to watch for TV reruns. Unfortunately, much of the spectacle and glory of these elaborate films fails to come across on the small screen.

However, you can relive the big-screen experience, in all its grandeur, in your mind's eye! Let's find out how well you remember as our quiz takes you back to all of those wonderful words and music.

Name that star!

(Male)

1. This famous star is best known for his dramatic roles. He was also a very able song-and-dance man and he won an Oscar for his leading role in *Yankee Doodle Dandy*.

FILM CREDITS: Footlight Parade *(1933)*
Yankee Doodle Dandy *(1942)*
The West Point Story *(1950)*
Love Me or Leave Me *(1955)*
The Seven Little Foys *(1955)*

Name that star!

2. A likeable and talented lanky dancer who is best remembered for his role in one of Hollywood's classic musicals.

FILM CREDITS: The Great Ziegfeld *(1936)*
The Wizard of Oz *(1939)*
Look for the Silver Lining *(1949)*
April in Paris *(1952)*
Where's Charley *(1952)*
Babes in Toyland *(1962)*

Name that star!

3. This singer-actor was a big star in musicals in the thirties and forties and then switched to dramatic, tough-guy roles.

FILM CREDITS: Forty-Second Street *(1933)*
Gold Diggers of 1935 *(1935)*
Thanks a Million *(1935)*
Stage Struck *(1936)*
On the Avenue *(1937)*
Star Spangled Rhythm *(1942)*

Name that star!

4. This dancer-singer-actor has had the longest and perhaps the most successful career in the history of Hollywood musicals.

FILM CREDITS: Roberta *(1935)*
Top Hat *(1935)*
Holiday Inn *(1942)*
Blue Skies *(1946)*
Easter Parade *(1948)*
Three Little Words *(1950)*
Finian's Rainbow *(1968)*

Name that star!

5. This fellow is a dancer-singer-comedian who was also a child star.

FILM CREDITS: Yes Sir, That's My Baby *(1949)*
The Milkman *(1950)*
Singin' in the Rain *(1952)*
Call Me Madam *(1953)*
There's No Business Like Show Business *(1954)*
Anything Goes *(1956)*

Name that star!

6. A great all-American type and all-around talent as a dancer-singer-actor.

FILM CREDITS: For Me and My Gal *(1942)*
Anchors Aweigh *(1944)*
Cover Girl *(1944)*
Ziegfeld Follies *(1946)*
Brigadoon *(1955)*
Les Girls *(1957)*

Name that star!

7. A big, tall song-and-dance man who starred in many musicals in the forties and fifties.

FILM CREDITS: Lady Be Good *(1941)*
Ziegfeld Girl *(1941)*
Panama Hattie *(1942)*
Mother Wore Tights *(1947)*
Give My Regards to Broadway *(1948)*
My Blue Heaven *(1950)*

Name that star!

8. An actor-singer-dancer who had a continental flair. His favorite prop was a straw hat. His favorite song was "Louise."

FILM CREDITS: Playboy of Paris *(1930)*
Love Me Tonight *(1932)*
The Merry Widow *(1934)*
Folies Bergère *(1935)*
Gigi *(1958)*
Can Can *(1960)*

Name that star!

9. One of America's top singing stars and for years a top recording artist, he did song, dance and comedy. He won an Oscar for a dramatic role in *Going My Way* (1944).

FILM CREDITS: Pennies from Heaven *(1936)*
Sing You Sinners *(1938)*
The Birth of the Blues *(1941)*
Blue Skies *(1946)*
The Bells of Saint Mary's *(1945)*
A Connecticut Yankee in King Arthur's Court *(1948)*

Name that star!

10. This talented actor was a song-and-dance man in the thirties. In recent years he has had two very successful TV series (one a comedy, the other a detective series).

FILM CREDITS: Captain January *(1935)*
Banjo on My Knee *(1936)*
Born to Dance *(1936)*
The Girl of the Golden West *(1938)*
My Lucky Star *(1938)*
Red Garters *(1954)*

Name that star!

11. A Hollywood star, he is one of America's top recording stars too. He has been known to do song-and-dance numbers with the best of them and has won acclaim for a number of dramatic roles in films.

FILM CREDITS: Anchors Aweigh *(1945)*
On the Town *(1949)*
Guys and Dolls *(1955)*
High Society *(1956)*
Pal Joey *(1957)*
Can Can *(1960)*

Name that star!

12. This famous singer-comedian was a blackface entertainer in the Ziegfeld Follies and then went to Hollywood.

FILM CREDITS: Whoopee *(1930)*
The Kid from Spain *(1932)*
Roman Scandals *(1933)*
Kid Millions *(1934)*
Show Business *(1944)*
If You Knew Susie *(1947)*

Name that star!

---

13. Often thought of as "the freckle-faced boy next door," this actor performed in MGM musicals as a song-and-dance man. He also appeared in a number of dramatic roles.

FILM CREDITS: Two Girls and a Sailor *(1944)*
Weekend at the Waldorf *(1945)*
Easy to Wed *(1945)*
Till The Clouds Roll By *(1946)*
In the Good Old Summertime *(1949)*
Brigadoon *(1955)*

Name that star!

14. This zany comedian and all-round entertainer was a very popular star in the forties and the fifties.

FILM CREDITS: Up in Arms *(1944)*
The Inspector General *(1949)*
Hans Christian Andersen *(1952)*
White Christmas *(1954)*
The Court Jester *(1956)*
The Five Pennies *(1959)*

Name that star!

15. A child star, this dynamic ball of energy became a talented actor-singer-dancer and comedian. (He is also an expert on marriage—or is it divorce?)

FILM CREDITS: Babes in Arms *(1939)*
Strike Up the Band *(1940)*
Babes on Broadway *(1941)*
Thousands Cheer *(1943)*
Girl Crazy *(1943)*
Words and Music *(1948)*

Name that star!

16. He became a romantic idol on his top-rated TV show which lasted many years. He's a singer who is a top recording artist. In films, he played in many comedies.

FILM CREDITS: My Friend Irma *(1949)*
At War with the Army *(1950)*
That's My Boy *(1951)*
The Stooge *(1952)*
Ten Thousand Bedrooms *(1957)*
Bells Are Ringing *(1960)*

Name that star!

17. He was a composer-lyricist-pianist and actor. His humor and biting wit, along with his deadpan delivery, gave us some of the finest moments in many a film.

FILM CREDITS: Rhythm on the River *(1940)*
Kiss the Boys Goodbye *(1941)*
Rhapsody in Blue *(1945)*
The Barkleys of Broadway *(1949)*
An American in Paris *(1951)*
The Band Wagon *(1953)*

Name that star!

18. A dynamic night club singer-dancer, a recording star and TV personality, this talented entertainer has appeared in only a handful of musicals.

FILM CREDITS: Porgy and Bess *(1959)*
Pepe *(1960)*
The Threepenny Opera *(1964)*
Sweet Charity *(1968)*

Name that star!

19. This talented Broadway dancer came to Hollywood and starred in many films in the thirties and forties. Years later, he left show business and went into politics.

FILM CREDITS: Kid Millions *(1934)*
Top of the Town *(1937)*
For Me and My Gal *(1942)*
Broadway Rhythm *(1943)*
This Is the Army *(1943)*
Show Business *(1944)*

Name that star!

20. His rich baritone voice and good looks made him a popular leading man in many musicals in the fifties.

FILM CREDITS: Tea for Two *(1950)*
On Moonlight Bay *(1951)*
By the Light of the Silvery Moon *(1952)*
The Desert Song *(1953)*
Oklahoma *(1955)*
Carousel *(1956)*

Name that star!

ADVENTURE-
SUSPENSE-
THRILLERS

Errol Flynn in *The Adventures of Robin Hood* (1938).

Humphrey Bogart and Ingrid Bergman in the classic *Casablanca* (1943).

Sean Connery as James Bond.

Left to right: Lana Turner,
Hedy Lamarr, Tony Martin
and Judy Garland in
Ziegfeld Girl (1941).

Ginger Rogers and Fred Astaire
in *Swing Time* (1936).

Kris Kristofferson and Barbra Streisand
in *A Star Is Born* (1976).

Gene Kelly doing his famous
dance in *Singin' in the Rain*
(1952).

George Raft and Marvin Miller in *Johnny Angel* (1945).

Basil Rathbone (as Sherlock Holmes) and Nigel Bruce
(as Doctor Watson) in *The Scarlet Claw* (1944).

Jean Harlow and James Cagney
in *The Public Enemy* (1931).

Edward G. Robinson in *Little Caesar* (1930).

Alan Ladd and Van Heflin in *Shane* (1953).
John Wayne and James Stewart in *The Shootist* (1976).

Randolph Scott, Errol Flynn
and Miriam Hopkins
in *Virginia City*
(1940).

Clint Eastwood in
Hang 'Em High
(1968).

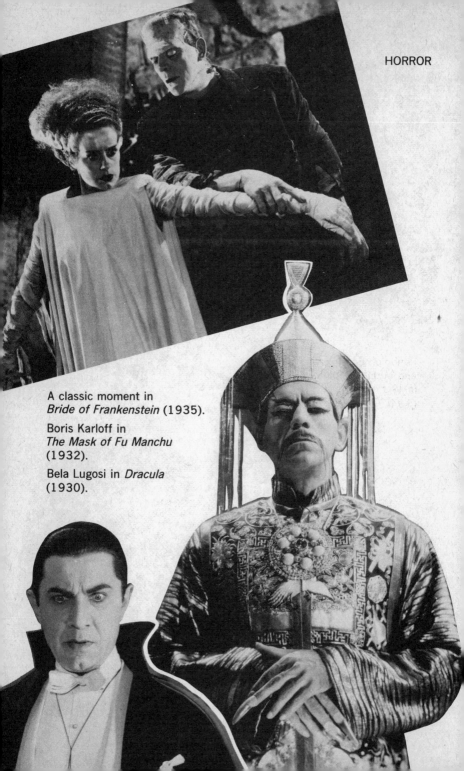

A classic moment in
Bride of Frankenstein (1935).

Boris Karloff in
The Mask of Fu Manchu
(1932).

Bela Lugosi in *Dracula*
(1930).

Name that star!

(Female)

1. Her real name was Frances Gumm, and throughout the forties she was one of Hollywood's top stars.

FILM CREDITS: Strike Up the Band *(1940)*
Ziegfeld Girl *(1941)*
For Me and My Gal *(1942)*
Meet Me in St. Louis *(1944)*
Till the Clouds Roll By *(1946)*
Words and Music *(1948)*

Name that star!

2. Primarily a dancer, she was perky and pleasant and appeared in many musicals in the forties and fifties, but never became a "big" star.

FILM CREDITS: Words and Music *(1948)*
Love Happy *(1949)*
On the Town *(1949)*
Three Little Words *(1950)*
Call Me Madam *(1953)*
White Christmas *(1954)*

Name that star!

3. She was as wholesome as apple pie and motherhood. One of the top stars of the fifties and also one of the nation's top recording stars.

FILM CREDITS: Young Man with a Horn *(1950)*
Tea for Two *(1950)*
I'll See You in My Dreams *(1951)*
April in Paris *(1952)*
Lucky Me *(1954)*
The Pajama Game *(1957)*

Name that star!

4. This gal became a star as a teenage soprano in the forties.

FILM CREDITS: Spring Parade *(1940)*
Nice Girl *(1941)*
It Started with Eve *(1942)*
Can't Help Singing *(1945)*
Up in Central Park *(1948)*

Name that star!

5. She was a dancer-actress who was one of the top pin-up girls of World War II.

FILM CREDITS: You'll Never Get Rich *(1941)*
The Strawberry Blonde *(1941)*
You Were Never Lovelier *(1942)*
My Gal Sal *(1942)*
Cover Girl *(1944)*
Pal Joey *(1957)*

Name that star!

6. An actress-singer-dancer, she was one of filmland's biggest stars in the thirties and forties. She is best remembered as the glamorous half of Hollywood's top dance team.

FILM CREDITS: Flying Down to Rio *(1933)*
The Gay Divorcee *(1934)*
Roberta *(1935)*
Top Hat *(1935)*
Lady in the Dark *(1944)*
The Barkleys of Broadway *(1949)*

Name that star!

7. She was a pretty singer of operatic range who starred in many MGM musicals in the forties and fifties.

FILM CREDITS: Rio Rita *(1942)*
Anchors Aweigh *(1945)*
Ziegfeld Follies *(1946)*
The Desert Song *(1953)*
Lovely to Look At *(1952)*
Kiss Me Kate *(1953)*

Name that star!

8. This blond actress-singer appeared in many Fox musicals in the thirties and forties.

FILM CREDITS: The King of Burlesque *(1935)*
On the Avenue *(1937)*
In Old Chicago *(1938)*
Alexander's Ragtime Band *(1938)*
Tin Pan Alley *(1940)*
Hello, Frisco, Hello *(1943)*

Name that star!

9. A very popular singing and dancing star who worked at the Fox studios. She was one of the top pin-up girls of World War II.

FILM CREDITS: Tin Pan Alley *(1940)*
Springtime in the Rockies *(1942)*
Sweet Rosie O'Grady *(1943)*
Coney Island *(1943)*
The Dolly Sisters *(1945)*
Mother Wore Tights *(1947)*

Name that star!

10. She was a comedienne-singer and a bundle of energy.

FILM CREDITS: Star Spangled Rhythm *(1942)*
And the Angels Sing *(1944)*
Incendiary Blonde *(1945)*
Duffy's Tavern *(1945)*
The Perils of Pauline *(1947)*
Annie Get Your Gun *(1950)*

Name that star!

11. An actress-dancer who had ballet training, she starred in many big MGM musicals in the forties and fifties.

FILM CREDITS: Till the Clouds Roll By *(1946)*
Words and Music *(1948)*
Singin' in the Rain *(1952)*
The Band Wagon *(1953)*
Brigadoon *(1955)*
Silk Stockings *(1956)*

Name that star!

12. A vivacious dancer-singer noted for her tap dancing ability, she was a featured player in many musical films and sometimes got top billing, too.

FILM CREDITS: Easter Parade *(1948)*
The Kissing Bandit *(1948)*
On the Town *(1949)*
Lovely to Look At *(1952)*
Kiss Me Kate *(1953)*
Hit the Deck *(1955)*

Name that star!

13. This pert performer was a singer-dancer-actress who became very popular in the fifties. Her big hit record was the name of a popular toy doll.

FILM CREDITS: Three Little Words *(1950)*
Singin' in the Rain *(1952)*
The Affairs of Dobie Gillis *(1953)*
Hit the Deck *(1955)*
Bundle of Joy *(1956)*
The Singing Nun *(1966)*

Name that star!

14. This fine female singer did feature numbers in quite a few big musicals in the forties.

FILM CREDITS: Panama Hattie *(1942)*
Cabin in the Sky *(1943)*
Broadway Rhythm *(1943)*
Stormy Weather *(1943)*
Ziegfeld Follies *(1946)*
Words and Music *(1948)*

Name that star!

15. Known as the "Brazilian Bombshell," this Latin singer was a popular featured star in musicals in the forties.

FILM CREDITS: Down Argentine Way *(1940)*
That Night in Rio *(1941)*
Week-End in Havana *(1941)*
Springtime in the Rockies *(1942)*
The Gang's All Here *(1943)*
Copacabana *(1947)*

Name that star!

16. Still very popular on TV today, this excellent soprano-actress starred in some big musicals.

FILM CREDITS: Oklahoma! *(1955)*
Carousel *(1956)*

April Love *(1957)*
Pepe *(1960)*
The Music Man *(1962)*

Name that star!

17. A top singing star of the stage who also made many films, she is noted for her powerful delivery.

FILM CREDITS: Kid Millions *(1934)*
Strike Me Pink *(1935)*
Anything Goes *(1936)*
Alexander's Ragtime Band *(1938)*
Call Me Madam *(1953)*
There's No Business Like Show Business *(1954)*

Name that star!

18. She wasn't really a singer or dancer, but MGM built a number of big musicals around her.

FILM CREDITS: Bathing Beauty *(1944)*
Easy to Wed *(1945)*
Take Me Out to the Ball Game *(1948)*
Neptune's Daughter *(1949)*
Jupiter's Darling *(1955)*

Name that star!

19. She is a French actress-dancer who had ballet training. After making some successful musicals, she turned to dramatic roles.

FILM CREDITS: An American in Paris *(1951)*
The Glass Slipper *(1954)*
Daddy Long Legs *(1955)*
Gigi *(1958)*

Name that star!

20. An American concert singer, she was a popular leading lady of the thirties.

FILM CREDITS: The Merry Widow *(1934)*
Naughty Marietta *(1935)*
Rose Marie *(1936)*
Maytime *(1937)*
The Girl of the Golden West *(1938)*
Sweethearts *(1939)*

Name that star!

Name that star!

Multiple choice

1. Who played the female lead in *Annie Get Your Gun* (1950)?
a. Betty Hutton   **b.** Betty Grable   **c.** Doris Day
d. Ann Miller   **e.** Vera-Ellen

2. The film cast of *Oklahoma!* (1955) was led by which male singer?
a. Dan Dailey   **b.** Gordon MacRae   **c.** Dennis Morgan
d. Howard Keel   **e.** Gene Kelly

3. Which actress starred with Rex Harrison in *My Fair Lady* (1964)?
a. Shirley Jones   **b.** Audrey Hepburn   **c.** Julie Andrews
d. Deborah Kerr   **e.** Florence Henderson

4. In the movie version of *The Music Man* (1962), who starred opposite Robert Preston?
a. Ann-Margret   **b.** Shirley Jones   **c.** Carol Lawrence
d. Debbie Reynolds   **e.** Shirley MacLaine

5. Barbra Streisand was the female lead in *Hello Dolly* (1969). Who was the male lead?
a. Frank Sinatra   **b.** Karl Malden   **c.** Ryan O'Neal
d. Walter Matthau   **e.** Bing Crosby

6. Name the star of *The Glenn Miller Story* (1954).
a. Larry Parks   **b.** Fred MacMurray   **c.** Robert Alda
d. James Stewart   **e.** Henry Fonda

7. *Funny Face* (1956) starred Fred Astaire and _____?
a. Rita Hayworth   **b.** Debbie Reynolds   **c.** Ginger Rogers
d. Leslie Caron   **e.** Audrey Hepburn

8. *Daddy Long Legs* (1955) starred Fred Astaire and _____?
a. Leslie Caron   **b.** Vera-Ellen   **c.** Ann Miller
d. Judy Garland   **e.** Ginger Rogers

9. Who starred with Gene Kelly in *An American in Paris* (1951)?
a. Doris Day   **b.** Leslie Caron   **c.** Cyd Charisse
d. Debbie Reynolds   **e.** Audrey Hepburn

10. *On a Clear Day You Can See Forever* (1969) starred Barbra Streisand and _____?
a. Yves Montand   **b.** Gene Kelly   **c.** Louis Jourdan
d. Tony Randall   **e.** George Segal

11. Who played the heroine in the Robert Wise-Jerome Robbins version of *West Side Story* (1961)?
a. Ann-Margret   **b.** Barbara Parkins   **c.** Shirley Jones
d. Connie Francis   **e.** Natalie Wood

12. *The Unsinkable Molly Brown* (1964) starred which leading lady?
a. Rosalind Russell   **b.** Doris Day   **c.** Shirley MacLaine
d. Lucille Ball   **e.** Debbie Reynolds

13. Who was the male lead in *South Pacific* (1958)?
a. Fernando Lamas   **b.** Gene Kelly   **c.** Rossano Brazzi
d. Ricardo Montalban   **e.** Gordon MacRae

14. Al Jolson starred in the legendary "first talking film," *The Jazz Singer*. Who starred in the 1952 remake?
a. Dan Dailey   **b.** Danny Thomas   **c.** Danny Kaye
d. George Murphy   **e.** Larry Parks

15. *Cover Girl* (1944) starred Gene Kelly and _____?
a. Lana Turner   **b.** Rita Hayworth   **c.** Betty Grable
d. Cyd Charisse   **e.** Alice Faye

---

16. Who played the romantic male lead in *Gigi* (1958)?
a. Rex Harrison   **b.** James Mason   **c.** Marlon Brando
d. Louis Jourdan   **e.** William Holden

17. In *High Society* (1956), who shared top billing with Bing Crosby and Frank Sinatra?
a. Judy Garland   **b.** Grace Kelly   **c.** Ava Gardner
d. Doris Day   **e.** Debbie Reynolds

18. Who starred with Howard Keel in *Show Boat* (1951)?
a. Kathryn Grayson   **b.** Janet Leigh   **c.** Betty Grable
d. Jane Powell   **e.** Judy Garland

19. Which actress starred in *Bye Bye Birdie* (1963)?
a. Sheree North   **b.** Tina Louise   **c.** Jill St. John
d. Ann-Margret   **e.** Mary Tyler Moore

20. *Looking For Love* (1965), starring Connie Francis, has as its claim to fame the only film appearance of one of the following famous talk show hosts. Which one was it?
a. Mike Douglas   **b.** Jack Paar   **c.** Johnny Carson
d. Merv Griffin   **e.** Phil Donahue

Name that movie!

1. This musical told the tale of a western heroine who was always getting into trouble.

THE CAST: Doris Day, Howard Keel, Allyn McLerie, Philip Carey, Gale Robbins

Name that movie!

2. This film was based on a Broadway play about "days of old when knights were bold."

THE CAST: Richard Harris, Vanessa Redgrave, Franco Nero, David Hemmings, Lionel Jeffries

Name that movie!

3. They might have titled this movie "The Dance in France"—but they didn't.

THE CAST: Frank Sinatra, Shirley MacLaine, Maurice Chevalier, Louis Jordan, Juliet Prowse

Name that movie!

4. This musical features a song that describes what people tend to do at the zoo.

THE CAST: Rex Harrison, Anthony Newley, Samantha Eggar, Richard Attenborough, Peter Bull

Name that movie!

5. The title of this movie is an American holiday tradition.

THE CAST: Fred Astaire, Judy Garland, Peter Lawford, Ann Miller, Jules Munshin

Name that movie!

6. This musical was about a famous writer of fairy tales.

THE CAST: Danny Kaye, Zizi Jeanmaire, Farley Granger

Name that movie!

7. This film told the story of a famous female café singer of the thirties.

THE CAST: Ann Blyth, Paul Newman, Richard Carlson, Rudy Vallee, Cara Williams

Name that movie!

8. The clue to the title of this musical is "a motel."

THE CAST: Bing Crosby, Fred Astaire, Marjorie Reynolds, Virginia Dale, Louise Beavers

Name that movie!

9. The story of famous song writer Gus Kahn, this movie has the same title as one of his most popular hit songs.

THE CAST: Doris Day, Danny Thomas, Frank Lovejoy

Name that movie!

10. It was just "fate" that brought this Broadway musical hit to the movie screen.

THE CAST: Ann Blyth, Howard Keel, Dolores Gray, Vic Damone, Monty Woolley

Name that movie!

11. The screen version of a Broadway hit by Cole Porter was based on *Taming of the Shrew*.

THE CAST: Howard Keel, Kathryn Grayson, Ann Miller, Bobby Van, Keenan Wynn

Name that movie!

12. This movie is the screen story of Cole Porter's life.

THE CAST: Cary Grant, Alexis Smith, Jane Wyman, Ginny Simms, Monty Woolley, Mary Martin

Name that movie!

13. This musical is the film version of a Broadway hit about three sailors in the "Big Apple."

THE CAST: Gene Kelly, Frank Sinatra, Jules Munshin, Ann Miller, Betty Garrett, Vera-Ellen

Name that movie!

14. This one's the screen version of a Lerner and Loewe Broadway biggie.

THE CAST: Jean Seberg, Clint Eastwood, Lee Marvin, Ray Walston, Harve Presnell

Name that movie!

15. The Gershwin story—but that's not the title.

THE CAST: Robert Alda, Joan Leslie, Oscar Levant, Paul Whiteman, Alexis Smith

Name that movie!

16. This screen musical was based on the Broadway show *No, No, Nanette,* though the title was changed.

THE CAST: Doris Day, Gordon MacRae, Gene Nelson, Eve Arden, Billy DeWolfe

Name that movie!

17. Gene did his most famous dance routine in this all-time favorite.

THE CAST: Gene Kelly, Debbie Reynolds, Donald O'Connor, Cyd Charisse

Name that movie!

18. This musical is the screen bio of George M. Cohan.

THE CAST: James Cagney, Joan Leslie, Walter Huston, Rosemary De Camp, Jeanne Cagney

Name that movie!

19. The Rodgers and Hart story is the subject of this musical. Clue: The title of this film tells how they worked together.

THE CAST: Tom Drake, Mickey Rooney, Perry Como, Mel Torme, Judy Garland, Betty Garrett, Lena Horne, Ann Sothern, June Allyson, Gene Kelly, Vera-Ellen, Cyd Charisse, Janet Leigh, Marshall Thompson

Name that movie!

20. This memorable musical featured some of Irving Berlin's best songs, and one of them was Bing's biggest hit.

THE CAST: Bing Crosby, Danny Kaye, Rosemary Clooney, Vera-Ellen, Dean Jagger

Name that movie!

True or false?

1. June Haver played Betty Grable's sister in *The Dolly Sisters* (1945).

2. *The Pirate* (1948) was a swashbuckler-musical that starred Douglas Fairbanks, Jr.

3. *Hello Dolly!* (1969) starred Ann-Margret.

4. Hollywood's two greatest male dancing stars, Fred Astaire and Gene Kelly, never appeared together in a film.

5. The star of *Alexander's Ragtime Band* (1938), a musical with no less than 26 songs, was Tyrone Power.

6. Ethel Merman starred with Natalie Wood in *Gypsy* (1962).

7. That fine operatic tenor who played romantic singing roles in the Marx Brothers films *A Night at the Opera* (1935) and *A Day at the Races* (1937) was Allan Jones.

8. The famous band leader who was featured in *Strike Up the Band* (1940) and *Rhapsody in Blue* (1945) was Tommy Dorsey.

9. The most popular pianist of the fifties and sixties, Liberace, never appeared in a musical film.

10. *The Birth of the Blues* (1941) starred Bing Crosby and Lena Horne.

11. The Disney Studios made many cartoon features that could be considered musicals: *Pinocchio, Fantasia, Peter Pan, Alice in Wonderland* and *Cinderella,* to name a few. However, the first full-length animated Disney musical to feature "live" actors was *Mary Poppins* (1964).

12. The actor who starred in *The Jolson Story* (1946) was Bert Parks.

13. The famous dancer who starred in *April in Paris* (1952) was Gene Kelly.

14. *Sweet Charity* (1968) starred Shirley MacLaine.

15. One of the stars of *How to Succeed in Business Without Really Trying* (1966) was that singing idol of the twenties, Rudy Vallee.

16. Frank Sinatra and Gene Kelly worked together in these three films: *Anchors Aweigh* (1945), *Take Me Out to the Ball Game* (1949) and *On the Town* (1949).

17. The female singer who starred in *Finian's Rainbow* (1968) was Ann-Margret.

18. *The King and I* (1956) starred Yul Brynner and Shirley Jones.

19. Richard Harris starred opposite Julie Andrews in *The Sound of Music* (1965).

20. *Gentlemen Prefer Blondes* (1953) starred Jane Russell and Marilyn Monroe.

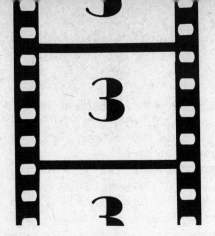

Gangster-Detective

How good is your memory of this bullet-spattered, action-packed film category? You'll soon find out! Perhaps you'll echo Sherlock Holmes and say, "Elementary, my dear Watson, elementary."

From *Little Caesar* (1930) to *The Godfather* (1971), gangster-detective films have dramatized murder and mayhem in bloody, vivid detail. But the old-fashioned gangster movie is a thing of the past. Hollywood has developed a "modern" image of today's gangster (and today's detective as well). Now we see films about scientific master criminals, international villains and spies, and almost superhuman secret agents.

Yet, the old gangster-detective movie tradition is still reflected in occasional films, such as *Dirty Harry, The French Connection,* and *Serpico,* and stars like Eastwood, McQueen and Bronson are our modern tough guys.

The old-time gangster-detective heroes are not out of the limelight, however. A strong "cult" following has developed around the old Bogart films and many theaters and TV stations continually run the old Bogart, Cagney, and Robinson films and many other early classics.

Name that star!

1. This tall, rugged actor played "good guys" and "bad guys." He appeared in westerns and war films and could always be counted on to turn in a strong performance.

FILM CREDITS: The Set-Up *(1949)*
The Racket *(1951)*
Beware My Lovely *(1952)*
House of Bamboo *(1955)*
Odds against Tomorrow *(1959)*
Dead or Alive *(1967)*

Name that star!

2. A very famous Hollywood tough guy, he started out in gangster roles and later proved himself to be one of filmdom's most versatile and competent talents.

FILM CREDITS: The Public Enemy *(1931)*
G-Men *(1935)*
Angels with Dirty Faces *(1938)*
Each Dawn I Die *(1939)*
The Roaring Twenties *(1939)*
White Heat *(1949)*

Name that star!

3. One of Hollywood's legendary tough guys, he proved to be a fine actor. Unfortunately, he is most remembered as a tough-guy type.

FILM CREDITS: Bullets or Ballots *(1936)*
The Last Gangster *(1938)*
Brother Orchid *(1940)*
A Bullet for Joey *(1955)*
Hell on Frisco Bay *(1955)*
The Biggest Bundle of Them All *(1967)*
(A couple of his biggest credits are omitted as they would be dead giveaways.)

Name that star!

4. He always played what he was, a smooth Italian-American from New York. Sometimes he was a cop, sometimes a killer; but he always turned in a taunt, believable performance.

FILM CREDITS: Call Northside 777 *(1948)*
Cry of the City *(1948)*
The Blue Gardenia *(1953)*
The Brothers Rico *(1957)*
Tony Rome *(1967)*
Lady in Cement *(1968)*

Name that star!

5. This burly actor, known as "the hunk," made his mark in several big costume films. He also starred in several gangster flicks.

FILM CREDITS: Kiss of Death *(1947)*
Cry of the City *(1948)*
The Las Vegas Story *(1952)*
Violent Saturday *(1955)*
Every Little Crook and Nanny *(1972)*

Name that star!

6. This husky, soft-spoken tough guy always managed to generate an atmosphere of danger and suspense around himself with his low-key acting style.

FILM CREDITS: Crossfire *(1947)*
Out of the Past *(1947)*
Macao *(1952)*
Thunder Road *(1958)*
Cape Fear *(1962)*
The Friends of Eddie Coyle *(1973)*

Name that star!

7. This long-time top star radiates sincerity and determination in every role he plays.

FILM CREDITS: Gilda *(1946)*
Framed *(1947)*
The Undercover Man *(1949)*
The Big Heat *(1953)*
The Blackboard Jungle *(1955)*
Ransom *(1955)*

Name that star!

8. Smooth, slick, but hard-bitten to the core—that was the kind of gangster role this famous tough guy played to the hilt.

FILM CREDITS: Scarface *(1932)*
Each Dawn I Die *(1939)*
They Drive by Night *(1940)*
Lucky Nick Cain *(1951)*
Black Widow *(1954)*
A Bullet for Joey *(1955)*

Name that star!

9. One of the greats! He played cynical tough guys who had a heart underneath it all. He wore a trench coat like a suit of armor against the cruel world his characters inhabited.

FILM CREDITS: The Petrified Forest *(1936)*
San Quentin *(1937)*
The Roaring Twenties *(1939)*
High Sierra *(1941)*
Dead Reckoning *(1947)*
Knock on Any Door *(1949)*

Name that star!

10. He was soft-spoken, tight-lipped and smooth. A major star of the forties and fifties, he played gangsters, detectives and soldiers of fortune.

FILM CREDITS: This Gun for Hire *(1942)*
The Glass Key *(1942)*
Lucky Jordan *(1942)*
The Blue Dahlia *(1946)*
Whispering Smith *(1948)*
Appointment with Danger *(1951)*
Hell on Frisco Bay *(1955)*

Name that star!

11. This square-jawed leading man was popular in the forties and fifties. He starred in a number of murder mysteries.

FILM CREDITS: Laura *(1944)*
Fallen Angel *(1945)*
Boomerang *(1947)*
Where the Sidewalk Ends *(1950)*
Edge of Doom *(1950)*
Beyond a Reasonable Doubt *(1956)*

Name that star!

12. This fine actress was a major star in the forties and fifties. She always played spirited, spunky women who were in trouble.

FILM CREDITS: The Adventures of Sherlock Holmes *(1939)*
They Drive by Night *(1940)*
High Sierra *(1941)*
Ladies in Retirement *(1941)*
On Dangerous Ground *(1951)*
Beware My Lovely *(1952)*

Name that star!

13. Rugged and athletic, this tough guy became a star in his first gangster movie. He has gone on to build a distinguished movie career playing action-adventure roles.

FILM CREDITS: The Killers *(1946)*
Desert Fury *(1947)*
Brute Force *(1947)*
Sorry, Wrong Number *(1948)*
Kiss the Blood Off My Hands *(1948)*
The Young Savages *(1961)*
Birdman of Alcatraz *(1962)*

Name that star!

14. A top-flight entertainer, he achieved fame as a song-and-dance man in films and then went on to dramatic roles, including a number of gangster-detective films.

FILM CREDITS: Suddenly *(1954)*
Ocean's Eleven *(1960)*
Robin and the Seven Hoods *(1964)*
Assault on a Queen *(1966)*
Tony Rome *(1967)*
Lady in Cement *(1968)*

Name that star!

15. A very competent character actor, heavy-set and always smoking a cigar or a pipe, he often played a corrupt politician or a police detective.

FILM CREDITS: Boomerang *(1947)*
Johnny O'Clock *(1947)*
On the Waterfront *(1954)*
Miami Exposé *(1956)*
The Garment Jungle *(1957)*
Party Girl *(1958)*

Name that star!

16. This stocky, powerfully built character actor always plays tough guys, whether they be hoods or cops. He probably has the deepest gravel-throated voice in the business.

FILM CREDITS: The Killers *(1946)*
Armored Car Robbery *(1950)*
The Narrow Margin *(1950)*
His Kind of Woman *(1951)*
Slaughter on Tenth Avenue *(1957)*
In Cold Blood *(1967)*

Name that star!

17. This blond actress played off-beat roles in gangster movies. She always yearned for attention, pouted and got treated badly.

FILM CREDITS: Crossfire *(1947)*
In a Lonely Place *(1950)*
The Big Heat *(1954)*
The Good Die Young *(1954)*
Human Desire *(1954)*
Odds Against Tomorrow *(1959)*

Name that star!

18. This fine actor started out as a "meanie," but worked his way into "good guy" roles. His weird laugh made him a star in his first movie.

FILM CREDITS: Kiss of Death *(1947)*
Road House *(1948)*
The Street with No Name *(1948)*
Night and the City *(1950)*
Panic in the Streets *(1950)*
Madigan *(1968)*

Name that star!

19. Smooth, suave and sophisticated is an accurate description of this tall actor who had a long and distinguished movie career.

FILM CREDITS: The Saint *(series; 1940–42)*
The Falcon *(series; 1941–43)*
Rage in Heaven *(1941)*
Hangover Square *(1944)*
The Lodger *(1944)*
Witness to Murder *(1954)*

Name that star!

20. This burly, hatchet-faced tough guy with a Brooklyn accent played soft-hearted thugs. He had a great flair for comedy, too.

FILM CREDITS: The Blue Dahlia *(1946)*
The Dark Corner *(1946)*
Calcutta *(1947)*
Race Street *(1948)*
The Big Steal *(1949)*
Detective Story *(1951)*

Name that star!

Name that star!

Multiple choice

1. Name the actress who starred opposite Burt Reynolds in *Shamus* (1972).
a. Ursula Andress **b.** Dyan Cannon **c.** Cybill Shepherd
d. Sally Field **e.** Raquel Welch

2. Who played the title role in *Johnny Eager* (1941), a gangster flick which also starred Lana Turner?
a. Robert Taylor **b.** William Holden **c.** David Janssen
d. Clark Gable **e.** Hugh O'Brien

3. Who played the lead in *Michael Shane, Private Detective* (1940)?
a. Van Johnson **b.** Ward Bond **c.** Lloyd Nolan
d. Macdonald Carey **e.** John Payne

4. Which of these "heavies" became a star playing the villian in *Kiss of Death* (1947)?
a. Lee Marvin **b.** Charles Bronson **c.** Richard Widmark
d. Dane Clark **e.** Ernest Borgnine

5. Who played the role of private eye Philip Marlowe in *Murder, My Sweet* (1944)?
a. Dick Powell **b.** Dennis Morgan **c.** Dana Andrews
d. Humphrey Bogart **e.** Robert Montgomery

6. Name the actor who starred in *Riot in Cell Block Eleven* (1954).
a. Neville Brand **b.** Charles McGraw **c.** Steve McQueen
d. Telly Savalas **e.** John Saxon

7. Who played the title role in *Al Capone* (1958)?
a. Leo Gordon **b.** Rod Steiger **c.** Brad Dexter **d.** Gilbert Roland **e.** Anthony Quinn

8. Name the actor who played detective Madigan in *Madigan* (1968).
a. Lloyd Bridges **b.** Richard Widmark **c.** Richard Conte
d. Cliff Robertson **e.** Robert Stack

9. Who was the popular actor who starred in *Cool Hand Luke* (1967)?
a. Jack Nicholson **b.** Paul Newman **c.** Ryan O'Neal
d. Robert Redford **e.** Clint Eastwood

10. Who starred in the classic *I Am a Fugitive from a Chain Gang* (1932)?
a. Lon Chaney, Jr. **b.** John Carradine **c.** Paul Muni
d. Wallace Beery **e.** James Cagney

11. A minor classic, *D.O.A.* or "Dead On Arrival" (1949), starred _____?
a. Edmond O'Brien **b.** Dana Andrews **c.** Gig Young
d. Alan Ladd **e.** Joseph Cotten

12. This heavy-set actor made his first film appearance as one of the murderers in *The Killers* (1946) and later went on to star as a detective in a TV series. What's his name?
a. Broderick Crawford **b.** Forrest Tucker **c.** Lee J. Cobb
d. William Conrad **e.** William Bendix

13. *Marlowe* (1969) brought the adventures of private eye Philip Marlowe back to the big screen. Who played the title role?
a. Robert Conrad **b.** Craig Stevens **c.** James Garner
d. Robert Wagner **e.** Ralph Meeker

14. Who created the title role of private eye in *Nick Carter, Master Detective* (1939)?
a. William Gargan **b.** William Powell **c.** Walter Pidgeon
d. Cary Grant **e.** Edmund Lowe

15. Speaking of "master detectives," who played the title role in *Ellery Queen, Master Detective* (1940)?
a. Chester Morris   **b.** Lloyd Nolan   **c.** Ralph Bellamy
d. George Montgomery   **e.** Robert Ryan

16. Who starred as the vicious killer in *Baby Face Nelson* (1958)?
a. Mickey Rooney   **b.** Eli Wallach   **c.** Audie Murphy   **d.** Dan Duryea   **e.** Barry Sullivan

17. Name the actor who starred in a dozen *Boston Blackie* films from 1941 to 1949.
a. George Raft   **b.** Lloyd Nolan   **c.** Chester Morris
d. Broderick Crawford   **e.** Dick Powell

18. Three different actors portrayed the Oriental detective Charlie Chan in a number of films. Two of these actors were Warner Oland and Roland Winters. Name the third.
a. Keye Luke   **b.** Peter Lorre   **c.** Claude Rains   **d.** Sidney Toler   **e.** Tony Randall

19. Bulldog Drummond is another famous film detective and many top actors played this role. Which one of the five actors listed below did *not* play Bulldog Drummond?
a. Ronald Colman   **b.** Ray Milland   **c.** Walter Pidgeon
d. James Mason   **e.** Ralph Richardson

20. Who played gangster Edward G. Robinson's girl friend in *Key Largo* (1948)?
a. Marie Windsor   **b.** Mary Beth Hughes   **c.** Ida Lupino
d. Claire Trevor   **e.** Joan Blondell

21. *The New Centurions* (1972) was the story of a veteran cop showing a rookie the ropes. Who starred with Stacy Keach in this one?
a. James Garner   **b.** Gene Hackman   **c.** Karl Malden
d. George C. Scott   **e.** Robert Blake

22. The 1973 remake of *Dillinger* starred Warren Oates. Who played the part of the FBI agent, Melvin Purvis, who nailed him?
a. Ben Johnson   **b.** George Kennedy   **c.** Cliff Robertson
d. Rod Steiger   **e.** Robert Stack

23. In the action-packed gangster film *The Getaway* (1972), who played the starring role?
a. Steve McQueen   **b.** Clint Eastwood   **c.** George Segal
d. Gene Hackman   **e.** Warren Beatty

24. Who played the girl friend of the violent hood in *White Heat* (1949)?
a. Claire Trevor   **b.** Virginia Mayo   **c.** Joan Blondell
d. Gloria Grahame   **e.** Alexis Smith

25. Who played the title role in *Machine Gun Kelly* (1958)?
a. Charles Bronson   **b.** Neville Brand   **c.** Peter Falk   **d.** Lee Marvin   **e.** Charles McGraw

26. *Murder, Inc.* (1960) starred Stuart Whitman and May Britt, but who co-starred as the mobster Abe Reles?
a. Eli Wallach   **b.** Lee J. Cobb   **c.** Ralph Meeker
d. Burgess Meredith   **e.** Peter Falk

27. Who played the role of the contract killer in *Hard Contract* (1969)?
a. Steve McQueen   **b.** James Coburn   **c.** Charles Bronson
d. Michael Caine   **e.** Robert Mitchum

28. Name the actor who played the title-role gangster in *The Rise and Fall of Legs Diamond* (1960).
a. Robert Ryan   **b.** Rod Steiger   **c.** Ray Danton
d. George C. Scott   **e.** Dan Duryea

29. *The St. Valentine's Day Massacre* (1967) starred _____?
a. Jason Robards, Jr.   **b.** Lee Marvin   **c.** Charles Bronson
d. Joe Don Baker   **e.** Lee Van Cleef

30. Name the actor who played the L.A. private eye in *Harper* (1966). His co-star was Lauren Bacall.
a. James Garner   **b.** Paul Newman   **c.** Robert Wagner
d. George Peppard   **e.** Burt Reynolds

31. The violent gangster thriller *Point Blank* (1967) starred a Hollywood tough guy. What was his name?
a. Richard Widmark   **b.** Lee Marvin   **c.** Lee Van Cleef
d. Clint Eastwood   **e.** James Coburn

32. Who starred in the film story of the hood who squealed on the Mafia? The name of the film was *The Valachi Papers* (1972).
a. Al Pacino   **b.** Lee J. Cobb   **c.** Jack Palance   **d.** Charles Bronson   **e.** Jason Robards, Jr.

33. Who starred in *House of Bamboo* (1955)?
a. William Lundigan   **b.** Robert Stack   **c.** Edmond O'Brien
d. Frank Lovejoy   **e.** Humphrey Bogart

34. Who co-starred with Jacqueline Bisset in the role of a Frisco police detective in *Bullitt* (1968)?
a. Clint Eastwood   **b.** Steve McQueen   **c.** George Segal
d. Warren Beatty   **e.** Paul Newman

35. *Serpico* (1973), the story of a New York cop, starred _____?
a. Gene Hackman   **b.** Don Murray   **c.** Al Pacino   **d.** Dustin Hoffman   **e.** Cliff Robertson

36. The 1972 film *Dollars($)* starred Goldie Hawn. Who co-starred?
a. Warren Beatty   **b.** James Coburn   **c.** Michael Caine
d. Steve McQueen   **e.** Lee Marvin

37. In *99 and 44/100 Percent Dead* (1974), the story of a gang war, who starred as the hired gun for one of the gangs?

a. Richard Harris b. Robert Mitchum c. Kirk Douglas
d. Burt Lancaster e. Charles Bronson

38. A taut gangster thriller, *The Narrow Margin* (1950) was the story of a policeman guarding a witness on a train from Chicago to Los Angeles. Who starred with Marie Windsor in this exciting film?
a. Broderick Crawford b. Charles McGraw c. Forrest Tucker d. Dana Andrews e. Edmond O'Brien

39. In Mickey Spillane's novel brought to the screen, *Kiss Me Deadly* (1955), who played the private eye Mike Hammer?
a. Ralph Meeker b. Frank Lovejoy c. Mark Stevens
d. Ray Danton e. Jack Palance

40. Who starred in *The Brotherhood* (1968)?
a. Marlon Brando b. Kirk Douglas c. Frank Sinatra d. Eli Wallach e. Richard Conte

Name that movie!

1. A beautiful girl is murdered—or so it seems. A police detective, while trying to find the murderer, falls in love with the girl. Clifton Webb achieved stardom in this one. A good story, fine performances and a great theme song all work to make this a classic.

THE CAST: Dana Andrews, Clifton Webb, Gene Tierney, Judith Anderson, Vincent Price

Name that movie!

2. Dirty doings down on the docks (what else is new?) and some powerful performances by a great cast make this film a winner. Unforgettable!

THE CAST: Marlon Brando, Eva Marie Saint, Lee J. Cobb, Rod Steiger, Karl Malden

Name that movie!

3. A group of famous detectives (of fiction) are brought together at the mansion of a wealthy recluse. A lot of murder, mystery and tongue-in-cheek comedy follow. Thin, but it works.

THE CAST: Peter Falk, Alec Guinness, Peter Sellers, Truman Capote, Estelle Winwood, Elsa Lanchester, Eileen Brennan, James Coco, David Niven, Maggie Smith, Nancy Walker

Name that movie!

4. This film was based on Graham Greene's novel *A Gun for Sale.* Alan Ladd and Veronica Lake light up the screen in this one.

THE CAST: Alan Ladd, Veronica Lake, Robert Preston, Laird Cregar, Tully Marshall, Pamela Blake

Name that movie!

5. A couple of war heroes are on their way to Washington to receive decorations when one of them disappears. The other begins tracking him down and uncovers his involvement with some hoods. The team of Bogart and Scott are worth the price of admission, even at today's prices.

THE CAST: Humphrey Bogart, Lizabeth Scott, Morris Carnovsky, Charles Crane, William Prince, Wallace Ford

Name that movie!

6. A police detective's wife is accidentally killed by a bomb planted to get him. He sets out to avenge her death by tracking down the mobsters responsible. Savage, tense thriller—the stuff good gangster movies are made of.

THE CAST: Glenn Ford, Gloria Grahame, Alexander Scourby, Jocelyn Brando, Lee Marvin, Jeanette Nolan, Carolyn Jones

Name that movie!

7. Boy meets girl. Boy and girl make frequent disputed bank withdrawals throughout the Midwest during the thirties. A two-popcorn-bag thriller; violent, but well done.

THE CAST: Warren Beatty, Faye Dunaway, Gene Hackman, Estelle Parsons, Michael J. Pollard, Dub Taylor, Denver Pyle, Gene Wilder

Name that movie!

8. A small-time professional bank robber discovers that he stole Mafia money on his last job. The mob begins to track him down, but he works out an elaborate scheme to outwit their hit man. Slick entertainment.

THE CAST: Walter Matthau, Joe Don Baker, Felicia Farr, Andy Robinson, John Vernon, Sheree North

Name that movie!

9. Con on "the rock" devotes "life time" to the study of birds. Good moments, but it gets "birdensome."

THE CAST: Burt Lancaster, Karl Malden, Thelma Ritter, Edmond O'Brien, Betty Field, Neville Brand, Hugh Marlowe, Telly Savalas

Name that movie!

10. Hoods hold a meeting in the Florida Keys, and some innocent folks are caught in the middle. A group of great pros take some ordinary material and make it tense and terrific!

THE CAST: Humphrey Bogart, Lauren Bacall, Claire Trevor, Edward G. Robinson, Lionel Barrymore, Thomas Gomez, Marc Lawrence

Name that movie!

11. A clergyman is killed in a quiet New England town. Enormous pressure is put on the D.A. to railroad a drifter for the crime. Instead, while prosecuting the case, the D.A. proves that the man on trial is innocent. An absolute classic of its kind.

THE CAST: Dana Andrews, Jane Wyatt, Lee J. Cobb, Cara Williams, Arthur Kennedy, Sam Levene, Taylor Holmes, Robert Keith, Ed Begley, James Dobson

Name that movie!

12. A neurotic, bedridden woman discovers that she is about to be murdered and tries to summon help by using the telephone. A ten-finger nail-biter!

THE CAST: Barbara Stanwyck, Burt Lancaster, Ann Richards, Wendell Corey, Ed Begley, Leif Erickson

Name that movie!

13. The story of two New York cops who decide to do a job for the Mafia. Instead of cowboys and Indians, we have this well-handled urban caper.

THE CAST: Cliff Gorman, Joseph Bologna, Dick Ward, Shepperd Strudwick, John P. Ryan, Ellen Holly

Name that movie!

14. An insurance agent collaborates with the beautiful wife of a client in a plot to kill her husband and collect. Gripping and great!

THE CAST: Fred MacMurray, Barbara Stanwyck, Edward G. Robinson, Jean Heather, Fortunio Bonanova, Porter Hall

Name that movie!

15. The exciting story of a tough D.A. who tracks down the leader of a gang who commits murders for a price. Clue: It's not *Murder, Inc.*

THE CAST: Humphrey Bogart, Everett Sloane, Zero Mostel, Ted de Corsia, Roy Roberts, King Donovan

Name that movie!

16. A tough Frisco police detective doesn't like to go by the book because the bad guys seem to get treated with kid gloves. When he goes after a vicious sniper-kidnapper he hands out justice in his own violent way. Police brutality well directed. A timely film that seems to touch the right nerve.

THE CAST: Clint Eastwood, Harry Guardino, Reni Santoni, John Vernon, Andy Robinson, John Larch

Name that movie!

17. Some vicious goons attack a businessman's wife and daughter. His wife is killed and his daughter is left in a state of permanent shock. The man decides to fight back against those who prey on defenseless people. He goes out, attracts muggers, and kills them. The critics' reaction: Who cares? But crime victims in audiences all over the country were standing up and cheering!

THE CAST: Charles Bronson, Hope Lange, Vincent Gardenia, Stuart Margolin, Stephen Keats, William Redfield

Name that movie!

18. The film story of Kate Barker, the outlaw, and her four sons. Murder and mayhem abound. This film set motherhood and apple pie back at least fifty years.

THE CAST: Shelley Winters, Pat Hingle, Don Stroud, Diane Varsi, Bruce Dern, Clint Klimbrough, Robert De Niro, Alex Cord

Name that movie!

19. Two likeable con artists get together in Chicago during the twenties and plot an elaborate scheme to get revenge on a mobster. This film is pure entertainment, including the theme song. A winner!

THE CAST: Paul Newman, Robert Redford, Robert Shaw, Charles Durning, Ray Walston, Eileen Brennan

Name that movie!

20. A tough, "I'll do it myself" kind of New York police detective picks up the trail of a consignment of drugs which has been smuggled into the country concealed in the floor of a car. A memorable performance by Hackman.

THE CAST: Gene Hackman, Fernando Rey, Tony LoBianco, Roy Scheider

Name that movie!

True or false?

1. That smooth sleuth of movies in the thirties and forties, Philo Vance, was played at various times by William Powell, Basil Rathbone, Paul Lukas and Alan Curtis.

2. The film *Sleuth* (1972) starred Michael Caine.

3. The private eye in *The Maltese Falcon* (1941) was named Philip Marlowe.

4. *The Notorious Lone Wolf* (1946) starred that suave actor Gerald Mohr.

5. In the 1959 remake of *The Hound of the Baskervilles,* the role of Sherlock Holmes was played by Christopher Lee.

6. *The Thin Man* and the sequels in this detective series of films starred Dick Powell and Myrna Loy.

7. *Chinatown* (1974) was a remake of an old Charlie Chan movie.

8. Private eye Peter Gunn was played by Craig Stevens in *Gunn* (1967).

9. Peter Lorre played the role of that famous oriental detective Mr. Moto.

10. Both Boris Karloff and Christopher Lee in their film careers played the role of Fu Manchu, the oriental master criminal.

11. In *The Brasher Doubloon* (1946), Humphrey Bogart played the private eye Philip Marlowe.

12. In *Brannigan* (1975), John Wayne played the role of a Chicago detective sent to London to bring back a gangster.

13. Hollywood never made a full-length feature film based upon the famous comic strip detective Dick Tracy.

14. Edward G. Robinson once played the role of a monk in a gangster film.

15. The star of *The Laughing Policeman* (1973) was Walter Matthau.

16. Donald Sutherland starred as the detective in the 1971 thriller *Klute*.

17. Roy Scheider, who played the local sheriff in *Jaws* (1975), had previously starred as a New York policeman in *The Seven-Ups* (1973).

18. Jan-Michael Vincent starred with Charles Bronson in *The Mechanic* (1972), a story about Mafia hit men.

19. The British comedy actor Nigel Bruce appeared as Dr. Watson in most of the Sherlock Holmes movies.

20. In *The Maltese Falcon* (1941), the actress who starred with Humphrey Bogart was Lauren Bacall.

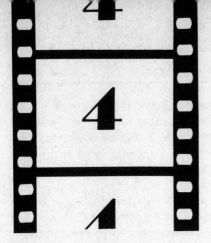

Westerns

It's time to pull on your boots, strap on your guns, climb into the saddle and ride out into the West of your memory to find out just how well you can score on the western section of The Great Movie Quiz.

Westerns have long been an important film-making category for Hollywood. Through the years, movie budgets have increased dramatically and many major stars have appeared in these bigger productions.

However, the western has been in a steep decline for the past ten years or so, with most of the "big star" productions being made overseas with actors like Eastwood, Bronson and

Van Cleef. And with the recent passing of the legendary John Wayne—the biggest and most durable western star of them all—the western may no longer be a regular film-production category for the studios. At present, there is no major star around who is dedicated to making westerns on a regular basis.

Of course, there will be John Wayne film festivals at local theaters around the land for years to come. And TV stations will also continue to show old westerns on a regular basis, enabling us to continue to enjoy the simple drama of the Old West.

Name that star!

1. One of Hollywood's top stars for over thirty years, he has played romantic leading men, and heroes in action-adventure films. He has also appeared in quite a number of westerns.

FILM CREDITS: The Man from Colorado *(1948)*
The Streets of Laredo *(1949)*
The Horse Soldiers *(1959)*
Alvarez Kelly *(1966)*
The Wild Bunch *(1969)*
Wild Rovers *(1971)*

Name that star!

2. This lanky actor has been a major star since the forties. He has played a wide variety of lead roles, including some notable westerns.

FILM CREDITS: The Yearling *(1946)*
Duel in the Sun *(1946)*
Yellow Sky *(1948)*
The Bravados *(1958)*
The Big Country *(1958)*
Mackenna's Gold *(1968)*

Name that star!

3. One of filmdom's tough guys, this dynamic actor has appeared in many action-adventure films.

FILM CREDITS: Apache *(1954)*
Vera Cruz *(1954)*
Gunfight at the OK Corral *(1957)*
The Professionals *(1966)*
Valdez Is Coming *(1971)*
Ulzana's Raid *(1972)*

Name that star!

4. He began his film career as a villain with a deadly sneer and crazy laugh. Later, he demonstrated his acting ability in a wide variety of dramatic roles.

FILM CREDITS: Garden of Evil *(1954)*
Broken Lance *(1954)*
The Law and Jake Wade *(1958)*
Warlock *(1959)*
The Alamo *(1960)*
Death of a Gunfighter *(1969)*

Name that star!

5. One of Hollywood's superstars, he has played in comedies, dramas, suspense films and westerns.

FILM CREDITS: Winchester 73 *(1950)*
Broken Arrow *(1950)*
Bend of the River *(1952)*
The Man from Laramie *(1955)*
The Man Who Shot Liberty Valance *(1962)*
Shenandoah *(1965)*
(He also starred in one of the great comedy westerns of all time.)

Name that star!

6. This handsome, rugged star appeared in a host of westerns, many of which were "B" productions. However, next to John Wayne, he was probably the best known western star of the forties and fifties.

FILM CREDITS: Western Union *(1941)*
Belle Starr *(1941)*
The Desperadoes *(1943)*
Badman's Territory *(1946)*
Fighting Man of the Plains *(1949)*
The Bounty Hunter *(1954)*
Plus many others

Name that star!

7. This Mexican-born leading man has turned in powerful performances in a variety of films, including some memorable westerns.

FILM CREDITS: The Plainsman *(1937)*
Union Pacific *(1939)*
The Ox-Bow Incident *(1943)*
Buffalo Bill *(1944)*
Ride Vaquero *(1953)*
The Man from Del Rio *(1956)*

Name that star!

8. This sleepy-eyed, soft-spoken star is considered one of Hollywood's famous tough guys.

FILM CREDITS: West of the Pecos *(1945)*
Track of the Cat *(1954)*
Bandido *(1956)*
The Wonderful Country *(1959)*
El Dorado *(1967)*
Villa Rides *(1968)*

Name that star!

9. This star is one of Hollywood's most famous heavies. He, John Wayne and Gary Cooper are the only actors who ever won Oscars (Best Actor) for their roles in a western.

FILM CREDITS: Bad Day at Black Rock *(1954)*
The Comancheros *(1961)*
The Man Who Shot Liberty Valance *(1962)*
Cat Ballou *(1965)*
The Professionals *(1966)*
Monte Walsh *(1970)*

Name that star!

---

10. This tall, mild-mannered actor made his mark as a star of many a western. He always liked to wear those big ten-gallon cowboy hats.

FILM CREDITS: Wells Fargo *(1937)*
Buffalo Bill *(1944)*
The Virginian *(1946)*
Four Faces West *(1948)*
Saddle Tramp *(1950)*
Ride the High Country *(1962)*

Name that star!

11. One of Hollywood's top stars, this leading man will always be remembered for his "heroic" roles in a number of big-budget productions.

FILM CREDITS: Pony Express *(1953)*
Arrowhead *(1953)*
The Far Horizons *(1955)*
The Big Country *(1958)*
Major Dundee *(1965)*
Will Penny *(1968)*

Name that star!

12. A durable top star, he has made more movies than anyone else who comes to mind.

FILM CREDITS: The Man from Colorado *(1948)*
The Man from the Alamo *(1953)*
Jubal *(1956)*
The Fastest Gun Alive *(1956)*
Cowboy *(1958)*
Heaven with a Gun *(1969)*

Name that star!

13. He has been a top star for over forty years and is considered one of Hollywood's immortals. He is soft-spoken, sincere and a fine actor.

FILM CREDITS: The Return of Frank James *(1940)*
The Ox-Bow Incident *(1943)*
My Darling Clementine *(1946)*
Fort Apache *(1948)*
The Tin Star *(1957)*
Welcome to Hard Times *(1967)*

Name that star!

14. This rugged, virile star has appeared in many big-budget action films.

FILM CREDITS: Man Without a Star *(1955)*
Gunfight at the OK Corral *(1957)*
Last Train from Gun Hill *(1958)*
The Last Sunset *(1961)*
Lonely Are the Brave *(1962)*
The War Wagon *(1967)*

Name that star!

15. This burly guy made his way to stardom by playing heavies. However, he has an Oscar to his credit for his portrayal of a "nice guy."

FILM CREDITS: Bad Day at Black Rock *(1955)*
Jubal *(1956)*
The Badlanders *(1958)*
Chuka *(1967)*
The Wild Bunch *(1969)*
Hannie Caulder *(1971)*

Name that star!

16. He's one of filmdom's top stars who usually plays a romantic leading man, often in light comedies.

FILM CREDITS: Tomahawk *(1951)*
Bend of the River *(1952)*
Horizons West *(1952)*
The Lawless Breed *(1952)*
Seminole *(1953)*
Showdown *(1973)*

Name that star!

17. This gaunt-looking actor usually plays villains. He became a star by playing just such a role in a western.

FILM CREDITS: Shane *(1953)*
The Professionals *(1966)*
The Desperadoes *(1969)*
Monte Walsh *(1970)*
The McMasters *(1970)*
Chato's Land *(1972)*

Name that star!

18. A tall, strong-featured leading man, he played in many types of films, including a number of westerns. He played the bad guy a bit more often than the good guy. Clue: His initials are R. R.

FILM CREDITS: Trail Street *(1947)*
Return of the Badmen *(1948)*
Bad Day at Black Rock *(1955)*
Day of the Outlaw *(1959)*
The Professionals *(1966)*
The Wild Bunch *(1969)*

Name that star!

19. This American superstar made his name appearing in several Italian westerns (but we won't list them).

FILM CREDITS: Star in the Dust *(1956)*
Ambush at Cimarron Pass *(1958)*
Hang 'Em High *(1968)*
Two Mules for Sister Sara *(1970)*
High Plains Drifter *(1973)*

Name that star!

20. A granite-faced tough guy, he was a featured player in films for many years and then suddenly emerged as a big star.

FILM CREDITS: Apache *(1954)*
Jubal *(1956)*
The Magnificent Seven *(1960)*
Lonely Are the Brave *(1962)*
Guns for San Sebastian *(1968)*
Chato's Land *(1972)*

Name that star!

Name that star!

Multiple choice

1. Who played the starring role in *One-Eyed Jacks* (1960)?
a. Clint Eastwood   **b.** Henry Fonda   **c.** Lee Marvin
d. Marlon Brando   **e.** Glenn Ford

2. *The Oklahoma Kid* (1939) starred two of filmdom's immortals; one was James Cagney. Name the other.
a. Clark Gable   **b.** Gary Cooper   **c.** Errol Flynn
d. Humphrey Bogart   **e.** Henry Fonda

3. Who starred in the 1966 western of revenge *Nevada Smith?*
a. Steve McQueen   **b.** James Stewart   **c.** Jack Nicholson
d. Randolph Scott   **e.** Chuck Connors

4. Who starred in that early big western classic *Cimarron* (1931)?
a. Tom Mix   **b.** John Wayne   **c.** Warner Baxter
d. Richard Dix   **e.** Wallace Beery

5. Who was James Stewart's leading lady in the western classic *Destry Rides Again* (1939)?
a. Claire Trevor   **b.** Jean Arthur   **c.** Anne Baxter
d. Marlene Dietrich   **e.** Maureen O'Hara

6. Who played the female lead in *Butch Cassidy and the Sundance Kid* (1969)?
a. Britt Ekland   **b.** Katharine Ross   **c.** Julie Christie
d. Ann-Margret   **e.** Kim Darby

7. Who starred with Lee Marvin in *Cat Ballou* (1965)?
a. Debbie Reynolds   **b.** Shirley Jones   **c.** Julie Bishop
d. Deborah Kerr   **e.** Jane Fonda

8. In the western classic *Shane* (1953), Alan Ladd played

the title role, but who played the homesteader who needed his help?
a. Ward Bond **b.** Van Heflin **c.** Robert Young **d.** Karl Malden **e.** Walter Brennan

9. In *The Cowboys* (1972), who killed John Wayne?
a. Bradford Dillman **b.** Gene Hackman **c.** Bruce Dern
d. Don Stroud **e.** Richard Jaeckel

10. Who starred in *Dirty Dingus Magee* (1970)?
a. Karl Malden **b.** Dean Martin **c.** Lee Marvin
d. Ernest Borgnine **e.** Frank Sinatra

11. Who played Gary Cooper's bride-to-be in that classic *High Noon* (1952)?
a. Dorothy McGuire **b.** Ellen Drew **c.** Grace Kelly
d. Barbara Rush **e.** Patricia Medina

12. *Stagecoach* (1939) made John Wayne a star. Who was the actor in that film who won an Oscar (Best Supporting Actor) for his role as the drunken Doc Boone?
a. Andy Devine **b.** Slim Pickens **c.** John Huston
d. Keenan Wynn **e.** Thomas Mitchell

13. Who starred in *McCabe and Mrs. Miller* (1971)?
a. Warren Beatty **b.** Steve McQueen **c.** Clint Eastwood
d. Jack Nicholson **e.** Cliff Robertson

14. Name the actress who starred in one of the early big westerns, *Union Pacific* (1939).
a. Jean Arthur **b.** Linda Darnell **c.** Claire Trevor
d. Alexis Smith **e.** Barbara Stanwyck

15. Who starred in *Little Big Man* (1970)?
a. Mickey Rooney **b.** Richard Dreyfuss **c.** Dustin Hoffman
d. Robert Conrad **e.** Red Buttons

16. Who starred with John Wayne in *El Dorado* (1967) playing the role of a drunken ex-lawman?
a. Ward Bond   **b.** Robert Mitchum   **c.** Dean Martin
d. Kirk Douglas   **e.** Lee Marvin

17. This well-known actress starred in a number of westerns. She always played a role in which she was as good as a man, or better. Some of her western film credits include: *Annie Oakley* (1935), *Union Pacific* (1939), *Cattle Queen of Montana* (1954), *The Violent Men* (1955) *Forty Guns* (1957). Which of these ladies are we talking about?
a. Anne Baxter   **b.** Barbara Stanwyck   **c.** Jean Arthur
d. Marie Windsor   **e.** Claire Trevor

18. Who was the noted dramatic actress who appeared in these three big westerns: *Dodge City* (1939), *Santa Fe Trail* (1940) and *They Died with Their Boots On* (1941)?
a. Donna Reed   **b.** Joan Fontaine   **c.** Joan Crawford
d. Olivia De Havilland   **e.** Deborah Kerr

19. Which one of these actors once played the Cisco Kid in a "B" western?
a. Cesar Romero   **b.** Anthony Quinn   **c.** John Wayne
d. John Carroll   **e.** Leo Carrillo

20. In *Pat Garrett and Billy the Kid* (1973), who played the role of Pat Garrett?
a. James Garner   **b.** Karl Malden   **c.** James Coburn
d. Stuart Whitman   **e.** William Conrad

21. Who played the title role in *Belle Starr* (1941)?
a. Audrey Long   **b.** Gene Tierney   **c.** Marie Windsor
d. Claire Trevor?   **e.** Barbara Stanwyck

22. *Streets Of Laredo* (1949) starred MacDonald Carey, William Holden and which one of these actors?
a. William Bendix   **b.** James Stewart   **c.** Robert Mitchum
d. Robert Ryan   **e.** Joel McCrea

23. Who played the title role in *Johnny Concho* (1956)?
a. Audie Murphy **b.** Jeff Chandler **c.** Frank Sinatra
d. Charles Bronson **e.** Richard Widmark

24. Name the star of a modern-day western *The Misfits* (1961).
a. Henry Fonda **b.** Gregory Peck **c.** Kirk Douglas
d. Burt Lancaster **e.** Clark Gable

25. In *The Westerner* (1940), who played the role of judge Roy Bean?
a. Lionel Barrymore **b.** Harry Carey **c.** Walter Brennan
d. William Demarest **e.** Dean Jagger

26. *Ride Vaquero* (1953) starred Robert Taylor, Anthony Quinn and which one of these actresses?
a. Barbara Stanwyck **b.** Ava Gardner **c.** Susan Hayward
d. Rita Hayworth **e.** Anne Baxter

27. *The Unforgiven* (1960) told the story of a girl suspected of being an Indian orphan. Who starred?
a. Audrey Hepburn **b.** Carroll Baker **c.** Ursula Andress
d. Martha Hyer **e.** Jeanne Crain

28. In *Sergeants Three* (1962), who starred along with Frank Sinatra and Dean Martin?
a. Jerry Lewis **b.** Peter Lawford **c.** Ben Johnson
d. Ward Bond **e.** Karl Malden

29. Who co-starred with Raquel Welch in *100 Rifles* (1969)?
a. Burt Reynolds **b.** James Stewart **c.** Dean Martin
d. Burt Lancaster **e.** Ernest Borgnine

30. The star of *A Man Called Horse* (1970) was _____?
a. Kirk Douglas **b.** Richard Harris **c.** Richard Widmark
d. Marlon Brando **e.** Yul Brynner

31. William Holden starred in *Wild Rovers* (1971). Who was his co-star?
a. James Caan   **b.** Ben Johnson   **c.** Ryan O'Neal
d. Don Murray   **e.** Glenn Ford

32. Which one of these stars did *not* portray General George Armstrong Custer in a western film?
a. Ronald Reagan   **b.** Errol Flynn   **c.** Robert Shaw
d. Richard Mulligan   **e.** Glenn Ford

33. One of these actors did *not* play the role of Buffalo Bill. Who is it?
a. Joel McCrea   **b.** Randolph Scott   **c.** Charlton Heston
d. Louis Calhern   **e.** Guy Stockwell

34. Jim Bowie was portrayed in westerns by all but one of these actors. Who never played Bowie?
a. Richard Widmark   **b.** Alan Ladd   **c.** Henry Fonda
d. MacDonald Carey   **e.** Sterling Hayden

35. Doc Holliday was played by nine different actors in various westerns. Which one of these actors did *not* play Doc?
a. Burt Lancaster   **b.** Victor Mature   **c.** Kirk Douglas
d. Jason Robards, Jr.   **e.** Walter Huston

36. Jesse James was another favorite character who was the subject of many westerns. All but one of the following actors played him. Who never played Jesse James?
a. Robert Ryan   **b.** Tyrone Power   **c.** Audie Murphy
d. Robert Wagner   **e.** MacDonald Carey

37. Wild Bill Hickok was the subject of his share of westerns, too. Which one of these actors never played this role?
a. Joel McCrea   **b.** Gary Cooper   **c.** Forrest Tucker
d. Rock Hudson   **e.** Bruce Cabot

38. More westerns were made about Billy the Kid than any other character of the West. Which one of these actors did *not* play Billy?
a. Paul Newman   **b.** Kirk Douglas   **c.** Roy Rogers
d. Johnny Mack Brown   **e.** Audie Murphy

39. The famous frontier marshal Wyatt Earp was also the subject of many westerns. Who never played Earp?
a. Henry Fonda   **b.** James Garner   **c.** James Stewart
d. Joel McCrea   **e.** Gregory Peck

40. Who starred in *The Honkers* (1971), a story about an aging rodeo star?
a. Glenn Ford   **b.** Randolph Scott   **c.** James Coburn
d. William Holden   **e.** Lee Marvin

Name that movie!

1. A Mexican village hires seven American gunmen for protection against bandits. This film has a great background theme and is often seen on TV.

THE CAST: Yul Brynner, Steve McQueen, Robert Vaughn, James Coburn, Charles Bronson, Horst Buchholz, Eli Wallach

Name that movie!

2. A modern western. A half-breed Vietnam veteran who returns home to Arizona roams the desert trying to protect the remaining wild mustangs and helps a runaway teenager.

THE CAST: Tom Laughlin, Delores Taylor, Bert Freed, Clark Howat, Ken Tobey

Name that movie!

3. The Cheyenne Indian tribe has been moved to a reservation 1,500 miles from their former home. Treated badly and unable to survive in this new location, they begin the long trek back "home." Score one for the Indians.

THE CAST: Richard Widmark, Carroll Baker, Karl Malden, Dolores Del Rio, Sal Mineo, Edward G. Robinson, James Stewart, Ricardo Montalban, Gilbert Roland, Arthur Kennedy

Name that movie!

4. The story of a poker game in which five rich poker players are tricked by a family of confidence artists. Clever and classy.

THE CAST: Henry Fonda, Joanne Woodward, Paul Ford, Jason Robards, Kevin McCarthy, Charles Bickford, Burgess Meredith

Name that movie!

5. A small-town marshal has a big decision to make. A group of tough outlaws are returning from prison to even the score with him and his town, and he must decide whether to stand against them alone or to run. Memorable—and vintage Cooper.

THE CAST: Gary Cooper, Grace Kelly, Thomas Mitchell, Lloyd Bridges, Katy Jurado, Lee Van Cleef

Name that movie!

6. Greed triumphs over the aspirations of three gold prospectors. A classic with strong performances by all.

THE CAST: Humphrey Bogart, John Huston, Tim Holt, Alfonso Bedoya, Bruce Bennett, Barton MacLane, Bobby Blake

Name that movie!

7. The shy, soft-spoken son of a famous gun-toting sheriff returns home to take over his late father's job. He tries to tame this wide-open town without using a gun. Pure entertainment—a classic!

THE CAST: James Stewart, Marlene Dietrich, Brian Donlevy, Charles Winninger, Jack Carson, Una Merkel, Allen Jenkins, Billy Gilbert

Name that movie!

8. Three wanderers are captured by a lynch mob and unjustly accused of a crime. A passing cowboy tries to stop the lynching but fails. Grim, but gripping and unforgettable.

THE CAST: Henry Fonda, Anthony Quinn, Dana Andrews, Jane Darwell, William Eythe, Mary Beth Hughes, Henry Morgan

Name that movie!

9. Buffalo Bill Cody and Wild Bill Hickok are given the job of establishing mail stations across the state of California. Certain interests, including some Indians, try to stop them. This is a "must" for the mailmen who think they have it tough today.

THE CAST: Charlton Heston, Forrest Tucker, Rhonda Fleming, Jan Sterling

Name that movie!

10. The beautiful wife of a wealthy rancher has been kidnapped. He hired a group of soldiers of fortune to get her back. A cast of pros.

THE CAST: Burt Lancaster, Lee Marvin, Robert Ryan, Jack Palance, Ralph Bellamy, Claudia Cardinale, Woody Strode

Name that movie!

11. A small-town sheriff has to deliver a prisoner to an incoming train at the local railroad station. He is menaced by the outlaw's friends and gets no help from the frightened townspeople. A simple but suspenseful western. We're all waiting for that train to pull in.

THE CAST: Glenn Ford, Van Heflin, Felicia Farr, Leora Dana, Henry Jones, Richard Jaeckel, Robert Emhardt

Name that movie!

12. Two well-known outlaws have numerous scrapes with the law. They finally flee to South America, where they meet their end at the hands of the law. A light-hearted, comic western with fine performances. It has turned out to be the biggest grossing western of all time!

THE CAST: Paul Newman, Robert Redford, Katharine Ross, Strother Martin, Henry Jones, Jeff Corey, Cloris Leachman, Ted Cassidy, Kenneth Mars

Name that movie!

13. The Duke, as an old cavalry officer who is about to retire, helps his command one last time when the chips are down. It is entertaining to watch the pros do their thing in fine style.

THE CAST: John Wayne, Joanne Dru, John Agar, Ben Johnson, Harry Carey, Jr., Victor McLaglen, Mildred Natwick, George O'Brien, Arthur Shields

Name that movie!

14. This movie tells the story of the first big cattle drive over the Chisholm Trail and the falling out between the leader of the drive and his foster son. A fine big western!

THE CAST: John Wayne, Montgomery Clift, Joanne Dru, Walter Brennan, Coleen Gray, John Ireland, Noah Beery, Jr., Harry Carey, Jr.

Name that movie!

15. There is lots of suspense and action in this story about Wyatt Earp's adventures in Tombstone and the battle with the Clantons at the OK Corral. A top cast makes this western a solid piece of entertainment.

THE CAST: Henry Fonda, Victor Mature, Walter Brennan, Linda Darnell, Cathy Downs

Name that movie!

16. In this John Wayne western, the Duke plays a Confederate war veteran who tracks down the Indians that killed his brother and sister-in-law and kidnapped their daughter. One of the Duke's better films.

THE CAST: John Wayne, Jeffrey Hunter, Natalie Wood, Vera Miles, Ward Bond, Henry Brandon, Harry Carey, Jr.

Name that movie!

17. This big western tells the story of two families who have been feuding over water rights for years. The feud ends when the heads of both families kill each other in a final showdown.

THE CAST: Gregory Peck, Jean Simmons, Charlton Heston, Carroll Baker, Burl Ives, Charles Bickford

Name that movie!

18. John Wayne plays a lone cavalry man who takes time away from his mission to defend a widow and her son from some marauding Indians. No one played John Wayne better than John Wayne, and he's always worth the price of admission.

THE CAST: John Wayne, Geraldine Page, Ward Bond, James Arness, Lee Aaker

Name that movie!

19. Two famous gunfighters decide to make a showdown between them pay off big, and so they sell tickets to the spectacle. The winner takes all, the loser gets buried. Thin, but it just manages to hold you right to the end.

THE CAST: Kirk Douglas, Johnny Cash, Karen Black, Raf Vallone

Name that movie!

20. This early western classic told the story of the American colonists who had to survive Indian attacks in upstate New York during the Revolutionary War. A great adventure western and a superb cast at their best.

THE CAST: Claudette Colbert, Henry Fonda, Edna May Oliver, John Carradine, Jessie Ralph, Arthur Shields, Robert Lowery, Ward Bond

Name that movie!

True or false?

1. *Jeremiah Johnson* (1972) starred Clint Eastwood.

2. Gary Cooper and Burt Lancaster once starred together in a western called *Vera Cruz* (1954).

3. James Stewart and John Wayne never starred together in a western.

4. William Holden once made a western with John Wayne.

5. Dean Martin starred with John Wayne in *Rio Bravo* (1959).

6. Rock Hudson and John Wayne never starred together in a western.

7. Tough guy and versatile actor Edward G. Robinson never appeared in a western.

8. Tom Mix starred in the original version of *Destry Rides Again* (1932).

9. Kirk Douglas once made a western with John Wayne.

10. In the history of the Academy Awards, no western has ever won the Best Picture award.

11. Jack Lemmon never starred in a western.

12. Charles Bronson and Henry Fonda once co-starred in a western.

13. Romantic movie idol Clark Gable never made a western.

14. The only westerns which Yul Brynner appeared in were *The Magnificent Seven* (1960) and *Return of the Seven* (1966).

15. One of John Ford's best films, *Wagonmaster* (1950), starred John Wayne.

16. *The Paleface* (1948) starred Bob Hope.

17. Elvis Presley never made a western.

18. John Wayne and Henry Fonda starred together in two war films, *The Longest Day* (1962) and *In Harm's Way* (1965), but they never made a western together.

19. Gary Cooper never made a western with either John Wayne or Henry Fonda.

20. Nearly every top male star in Hollywood has made one or more westerns. The list includes Glenn Ford, William Holden, Robert Taylor, Clark Gable, Tyrone Power, James Stewart, Spencer Tracy, Humphrey Bogart, James Cagney, Alan Ladd, Edward G. Robinson, Henry Fonda, Kirk Douglas, Rock Hudson, Paul Newman, Robert Redford, Burt Lancaster and Gregory Peck. One major star is an outstanding exception—Cary Grant never made a western.

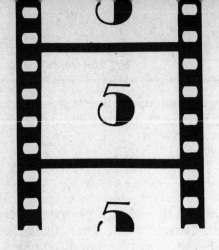

Horror

Remember how many times you were scared out of your wits, in spite of yourself, by some silly horror flick? It's happened to all of us—and it's a lot of fun!

The grand old horror films of Lugosi and Karloff can never be topped. They still play with regularity in many theaters and are constantly shown on TV. Such great stars as Price, Lee and Cushing have been very busy grinding out remakes of the oldies and finding new horror vehicles.

In the past decade, a new genre of horror film has come into vogue. Instead of monsters and mad scientists, we have stories about the occult and witchcraft. Films like *The Exorcist* and *The Omen* are tailored for a much wider audience, and they have captured it.

Now, let's find out how "horrorable" your memory is.

Name that star!

1. This tall, suave actor has played in many different kinds of films, but he has also made a name for himself as one of the most prominent and durable stars of horror movies.

FILM CREDITS: The Fall of the House of Usher *(1961)*
The Pit and the Pendulum *(1961)*
Tales of Terror *(1962)*
The Raven *(1963)*
Cry of the Banshee *(1970)*
Theatre of Blood *(1973)*

Name that star!

2. This British actor became a star playing character roles in many notable horror flicks. Today, he is one of the most popular actors appearing in this genre of films.

FILM CREDITS: The Mummy *(1959)*
Brides of Dracula *(1960)*
Torture Garden *(1967)*
I, Monster *(1970)*
Tales from the Crypt *(1971)*
Fear in the Night *(1972)*

Name that star!

3. A gaunt American actor, he is capable of playing Shakespeare on the stage, but is finding steady work playing mad doctors and the like in horror films.

FILM CREDITS: Bride of Frankenstein *(1935)*
Bluebeard *(1944)*
House of Frankenstein *(1945)*
The Cosmic Man *(1959)*
The Fiend with the Electronic Brain *(1967)*
House of the Seven Corpses *(1973)*

Name that star!

4. This hulking actor began to make his mark in horror films when he played the role of Larry Talbot in *The Wolf Man*.

FILM CREDITS: The Wolf Man *(1941)*
The Ghost of Frankenstein *(1942)*
The Mummy's Tomb *(1942)*
Frankenstein Meets the Wolf Man *(1943)*
Son of Dracula *(1943)*
House of Frankenstein *(1945)*

Name that star!

5. This tall British actor has made quite a career for himself starring in horrors; in fact, in recent years he has probably made more horror films than anyone else in the business.

FILM CREDITS: The Hands of Orlac *(1960)*
Dr. Terror's House of Horrors *(1963)*
The Skull *(1965)*
The Face of Fu Manchu *(1965)*
Rasputin the Mad Monk *(1965)*
I Monster *(1971)*

Name that star!

6. His rolling eyes and sinister voice made him a "natural" for suspense-horror roles. He seemed meek, but deadly.

FILM CREDITS: Island of Doomed Men *(1940)*
The Boogie Man Will Get You *(1942)*
The Beast with Five Fingers *(1946)*
Tales of Terror *(1962)*
The Raven *(1963)*
Comedy of Terrors *(1963)*

Name that star!

7. He always played the mad doctor/scientist roles and gave them some class with his British accent and dignified manner.

FILM CREDITS: The Mummy's Hand *(1940)*
Dead Men Walk *(1943)*
The Black Raven *(1943)*
The Mad Ghoul *(1943)*
House of Frankenstein *(1945)*
Fog Island *(1945)*

Name that star!

8. This British leading lady is one of the few actresses who specialized in starring horror roles. Clue: She shares the last name of the lady who wrote the novel *Frankenstein*.

FILM CREDITS: Blood of the Vampire *(1959)*
Village of the Damned *(1961)*
Shadow of the Cat *(1962)*
The Gorgon *(1964)*
The Secret of Blood Island *(1965)*
Rasputin the Mad Monk *(1965)*

Name that star!

9. This sharp-featured British actor played an excellent villain in a variety of films. He also portrayed a famous British detective.

FILM CREDITS: Son of Frankenstein *(1939)*
Tower of London *(1940)*
House of Fear *(1943)*
The Scarlet Claw *(1944)*
The Black Sleep *(1957)*
Tales of Terror *(1962)*

Name that star!

NAME THAT STAR! • 103

10. This versatile actor has a flair for comedy as well as for playing villains. He appeared in the title role of the remake of *The Phantom of the Opera*.

FILM CREDITS: Mysterious Island *(1961)*
Phantom of the Opera *(1962)*
Murders in the Rue Morgue *(1971)*
Asylum *(1972)*
And Now the Screaming Starts *(1973)*

Name that star!

11. This distinguished German character actor has portrayed some memorable villains in a variety of films.

FILM CREDITS: The Cabinet of Dr. Caligari *(1919)*
Waxworks *(1924)*
Lucrezia Borgia *(1925)*
Rasputin *(1930)*
King of the Damned *(1935)*
The Thief of Baghdad *(1940)*

Name that star!

12. This well-known Hollywood star has had a long and successful career in films. He has appeared in several horror flicks; unfortunately none of them were of high caliber.

FILM CREDITS: The Premature Burial *(1962)*
The Man with X-Ray Eyes*(1963)*
Frogs *(1972)*
The Thing with Two Heads *(1972)*
Terror in the Wax Museum *(1973)*
The House in Nightmare Park *(1973)*

Name that star!

13. This British character actor has played many villains and mad doctors, often wearing a monocle. He also played the arch-criminal Professor Moriarty in a Sherlock Holmes film.

FILM CREDITS: Doctor X *(1932)*
The Vampire Bat *(1933)*
Mark of the Vampire *(1935)*
Man Made Monster *(1941)*
The Mad Doctor of Market Street *(1942)*
House of Frankenstein *(1945)*

Name that star!

14. This tall, dapper leading man from Britain played private investigators and adventurers in many "B" films. He also appeared in a number of horror flicks.

FILM CREDITS: Cat People *(1942)*
I Walked with a Zombie *(1943)*
The Seventh Victim *(1943)*
The She-Creature *(1956)*
Voodoo Woman *(1957)*

Name that star!

15. This fellow is a British character actor who, late in his career, came to Hollywood and played sour-faced bumbling butlers and burgomasters in a number of excellent horror films.

FILM CREDITS: The Mystery of Edwin Drood *(1935)*
Bride of Frankenstein *(1935)*
Dracula's Daughter *(1936)*
Night Must Fall *(1937)*
The Hound of the Baskervilles *(1939)*

Name that star!

NAME THAT STAR! • 105

16. He is one of the immortals of horror films (so long as no one drives a wooden stake into his heart).

FILM CREDITS: Dracula *(1930)*
The Murders in the Rue Morgue *(1931)*
White Zombie *(1932)*
Chandu the Magician *(1932)*
The Black Cat *(1934)*
Son of Frankenstein *(1939)*
And many, many others

Name that star!

17. This heavy-browed, gaunt British character actor has achieved lasting fame as the principal player in a great many classic horror films. (His name is a household scream.)

FILM CREDITS: Bride of Frankenstein *(1935)*
The Raven *(1935)*
Tower of London *(1939)*
The Body Snatcher *(1945)*
House of Frankenstein *(1945)*
The Black Castle *(1952)*
And many, many others

Name that star!

18. This American character actor was short of stature, but long on acting ability. He appeared in a variety films, including some great horror flicks. On TV, he starred in two series, *Life with Luigi* and *Charlie Chan.*

FILM CREDITS: Island of Lost Men *(1939)*
Dr. Renault's Secret *(1942)*
The Monster Maker *(1944)*
House Of Frankenstein *(1945)*
The Beast with Five Fingers *(1946)*
Dracula vs. Frankenstein *(1971)*

Name that star!

19. This beautiful red-headed English actress has made a career out of playing high-bred ladies who are involved with madmen in these horror operas.

FILM CREDITS: Ghost Ship *(1952)*
The Curse of Frankenstein *(1956)*
The Man Who Could Cheat Death *(1959)*
Doctor Blood's Coffin *(1960)*
The Premature Burial *(1962)*
The Masque of the Red Death *(1964)*

Name that star!

20. This British leading lady of the horrors has played witches, vampires and strange women in a number of foreign-made chillers.

FILM CREDITS: The Pit and the Pendulum *(1961)*
The Terror of Dr. Hitchcock *(1962)*
Castle of Blood *(1963)*
The Spectre *(1964)*
Terror-Creature from the Grave *(1965)*
The Revenge of the Blood Beast *(1965)*

Name that star!

Name that star!

Multiple choice

1. Who starred in the 1962 remake of *The Phantom of the Opera?*
a. Herbert Lom   **b.** Vincent Price   **c.** Paul Henreid
d. Louis Jourdan   **e.** Christopher Lee

2. A popular American character actor starred in the horror thriller *Sssss* (1973). What was his name?
a. Burl Ives   **b.** Ben Johnson   **c.** Strother Martin   **d.** Martin Balsam   **e.** Red Buttons

3. Name the famous actor who won an Academy Award for his title roles in *Dr. Jekyll and Mr. Hyde* (1932).
a. Fredric March   **b.** Spencer Tracy   **c.** John Barrymore
d. John Huston   **e.** Lon Chaney

4. Who co-starred with Bette Davis in *What Ever Happened to Baby Jane?* (1962)?
a. Shelley Winters   **b.** Olivia De Havilland   **c.** Joan Crawford   **d.** Ida Lupino   **e.** Angela Lansbury

5. Bette Davis starred in another horror thriller, *Hush . . . Hush, Sweet Charlotte* (1964). Who was her co-star in this film?
a. Celeste Holm   **b.** Joan Fontaine   **c.** Barbara Stanwyck
d. Susan Hayward   **e.** Olivia De Havilland

6. Who starred with Boris Karloff and Bela Lugosi in *Son of Frankenstein* (1939)?
a. Basil Rathbone   **b.** Lionel Atwill   **c.** John Carradine
d. Lionel Barrymore   **e.** Peter Lorre

7. Who played the title role in *The Werewolf of London* (1935)?
a. Boris Karloff   **b.** Henry Hull   **c.** J. Carrol Naish   **d.** Lon Chaney, Jr.   **e.** John Carradine

8. Who played the famous role of Igor in *Son of Frankenstein* (1939)?
a. Bela Lugosi **b.** Boris Karloff **c.** Charles Laughton
d. J. Carrol Naish **e.** Vincent Price

9. Who starred in *Curse of the Werewolf* (1961)?
a. Vincent Price **b.** Oliver Reed **c.** Peter Cushing
d. Christopher Lee **e.** Lon Chaney, Jr.

10. Name the star of the horror flick *The Mephisto Waltz* (1971).
a. Alan Alda **b.** George Segal **c.** Ray Milland **d.** Ryan O'Neal **e.** William Holden

11. *Psychomania* (1972) was a chiller about a Hell's Angels motorcyclist who returns from the dead as a monster that cannot be killed. Who starred in this nightmare?
a. George Sanders **b.** Christopher Lee **c.** Patrick Magee
d. Roddy McDowall **e.** Marlon Brando

12. Name the well-known actress who starred in *Baron Blood* (1972).
a. Barbara Parkins **b.** Virna Lisi **c.** Jane Fonda **d.** Elke Sommer **e.** Shelley Winters

13. Who played the sinister doctor in *Torture Garden* (1968), which also starred Jack Palance and Peter Cushing?
a. Christopher Lee **b.** Strother Martin **c.** Vincent Price
d. Burgess Meredith **e.** Stephen McNally

14. Who starred in *Revenge of the Zombies* (1943)?
a. John Carradine **b.** Claude Rains **c.** Lon Chaney, Jr.
d. Boris Karloff **e.** Bela Lugosi

15. The famous Hollywood tough guy who appeared in *The Return of Dr. X* (1939) was _____?

a. George Raft **b.** Humphrey Bogart **c.** Edward G. Robinson **d.** Paul Muni **e.** James Cagney

16. *The Premature Burial* (1962) starred a well-known Hollywood actor who made several horror films in the sixties and seventies. What was his name?
a. Rock Hudson **b.** Ray Milland **c.** Rod Taylor **d.** Roddy McDowall **e.** Jason Robards, Jr.

17. Who starred as Vincent Price's brother in *The Oblong Box* (1969)?
a. Christopher Lee **b.** Peter Cushing **c.** George Sanders **d.** Tom Conway **e.** James Mason

18. Name the famous Hollywood actor who starred in *The Nightcomers* (1971).
a. Ray Milland **b.** Gregory Peck **c.** Marlon Brando **d.** Charlton Heston **e.** Glenn Ford

19. *Monster from Green Hell* (1957) starred a lanky actor who is often seen in westerns. What is his name?
a. Jim Davis **b.** Joel McCrea **c.** Charles Coburn **d.** Clint Eastwood **e.** Robert Ryan

20. *Not of This Earth* (1958) is a story about vampires from outer space. Name the actress who starred in it.
a. Mari Blanchard **b.** Beverly Garland **c.** Julie Adams **d.** Julie London **e.** Mary Murphy

21. Which one of these actresses starred with Ben Johnson and Robert Armstrong in *Mighty Joe Young* (1949)?
a. Margaret O'Brien **b.** Marie Wilson **c.** Terry Moore **d.** June Lockhart **e.** Marie McDonald

22. Who starred in the thriller based on the stories of Edgar Allan Poe, *The Masque of the Red Death* (1964)?
a. Vincent Price **b.** Claude Rains **c.** Sydney Greenstreet **d.** Christopher Lee **e.** Boris Karloff

23. Detective Mike Shayne encounters a criminal who has returned to life in *The Man Who Wouldn't Die* (1942). Who played Mike Shayne in this one?
a. Chester Morris   **b.** Wayne Morris   **c.** Broderick Crawford
d. Lloyd Nolan   **e.** Pat O'Brien

24. Who played the title role in *The Mad Doctor* (1940)?
a. Basil Rathbone   **b.** George Zucco   **c.** George Macready
d. Peter Lorre   **e.** Charles Laughton

25. In *The Lodger* (1944), the story of Jack the Ripper, who played the title role and co-starred with Merle Oberon and George Sanders?
a. Laird Cregar   **b.** Sydney Greenstreet   **c.** Vincent Price
d. Herbert Lom   **e.** Herbert Marshall

26. Who starred in *The Legend of Hell House* (1973)?
a. Peter Lawford   **b.** Chuck Connors   **c.** William Holden
d. Jackie Cooper   **e.** Roddy McDowall

27. In *The Evil of Frankenstein* (1964), who played Dr. Frankenstein?
a. Boris Karloff   **b.** Christopher Lee   **c.** Vincent Price
d. Peter Cushing   **e.** Patrick Magee

28. In the old classic *Fog Island* (1945), who co-starred with Lionel Atwill?
a. George Zucco   **b.** Basil Rathbone   **c.** John Carradine
d. Lon Chaney, Jr.   **e.** Elisha Cook, Jr.

29. *Eye of the Devil* (1967) starred two famous Hollywood players who have appeared together in several films. David Niven was one. Who was the other?
a. Maureen O'Hara   **b.** Deborah Kerr   **c.** Joan Fontaine
d. Olivia De Havilland   **e.** Bette Davis

30. In a switch from her usual light teenage romance films, this actress starred in *The Dunwich Horror* (1969). Who was it?
a. Ann-Margret **b.** Sandra Dee **c.** Annette Funicello
d. Margaret O'Brien **e.** Kim Darby

31. Who starred in *Dracula, Prince of Darkness* (1965), which was a sequel to *Horror of Dracula?*
a. Tom Conway **b.** George Sanders **c.** Christopher Lee
d. Vincent Price **e.** Jack Palance

32. *Don't Look Now* (1973)—the story of a couple in Venice who, while searching for their lost daughter, encounter an eerie psychic force—starred Julie Christie. Who was her co-star?
a. Gregory Peck **b.** William Holden **c.** Donald Sutherland
d. George Segal **e.** Warren Beatty

33. The old classic horror thriller *Dr. X* (1932) starred Preston Foster, and Lionel Atwill played the doctor. Who played the tough investigative reporter who nails the doctor?
a. Lloyd Nolan **b.** Lee Tracy **c.** Robert Armstrong
d. Brian Donlevy **e.** Chester Morris

34. *The Diary of a Madman* (1963) was based on a story by Guy de Maupassant. Who starred?
a. Vincent Price **b.** George Sanders **c.** Herbert Marshall
d. Robert Morley **e.** Zachary Scott

35. Who starred with Boris Karloff in *Die, Monster, Die* (1965)?
a. Mickey Rooney **b.** Steve McQueen **c.** Roddy McDowall
d. Robert Wagner **e.** Nick Adams

36. In a minor horror classic, *The Devil Doll* (1936), a mad scientist decides that the world would be a better place if it were inhabited by humans six inches tall, and he dispatches

a band of mini-killers to do away with his immediate enemies.
Who played the role of this mad scientist?
a. Lionel Barrymore   b. Lon Chaney   c. John Carradine
d. John Barrymore   e. Lionel Atwill

37. Who starred in *Dr. Terror's House of Horrors* (1965)?
a. Christopher Lee   b. Vincent Price   c. Peter Cushing
d. Boris Karloff   e. Herbert Lom

38. The classic horror film *Isle of the Dead* (1945) starred
_____?
a. Bela Lugosi   b. Boris Karloff   c. Peter Lorre   d. Lionel
Barrymore   e. George Sanders

39. An excellent horror classic, *The Creeping Unknown*
(1956) inspired a couple of sequels. Who starred in this hair-
straightener?
a. Forrest Tucker   b. John Agar   c. Brian Donlevy   d. Lew
Ayres   e. Ralph Bellamy

40. Who starred in *Chamber of Horrors* (1966) along with
Wilfrid Hyde-White, Cesare Danova and Tony Curtis?
a. Patrick O'Neal   b. Vincent Price   c. Terry-Thomas
d. Peter Sellers   e. Joseph Cotten

Name that movie!

1. A sculptor is badly burned when his wax museum goes up in flames and he is no longer able to sculpt. Nevertheless, he starts another wax museum. This time his exhibits are real people whom he has murdered and preserved in wax. Price waxes eloquent as usual.

THE CAST: Vincent Price, Phyllis Kirk, Frank Lovejoy, Charles Bronson, Carolyn Jones, Paul Cavanagh

Name that movie!

2. Giant crabs attack a group of scientists who are trapped on a desolate Pacific island. A lot of claws, but no meat to this one. A classic clinker!

THE CAST: Richard Garland, Pamela Duncan, Russell Johnson, Leslie Bradley

Name that movie!

3. An army of rats (rodents, not people) attempts to take over a city. The Pied Piper not being available, the U.S. Army moves in to do battle. This film was a sequel to *Willard*—did we need one?

THE CAST: Joseph Campanella, Arthur O'Connell, Meredith Baxter, Lee Harcourt Montgomery, Rosemary Murphy

Name that movie!

4. A man marries a woman who comes from a European town where an ancient curse causes all of the women to change into vicious cats (the jungle variety) whenever they get upset. A thriller, and perhaps even a classic of its kind.

THE CAST: Kent Smith, Simone Simon, Tom Conway, Jane Randolph, Elizabeth Russell, Jack Holt

Name that movie!

5. A missing link climbs out of the drink! A strange "gillman" leaves his lagoon in the Amazon jungle and proceeds to try to annihilate the members of a scientific expedition. If you let yourself go (as you surely should when viewing a horror film), it's quite watchable.

THE CAST: Richard Carlson, Julia Adams, Richard Denning, Antonio Moreno

Name that movie!

6. A rich musical genius (who lost his face in an car accident) wants revenge on a team of surgeons who let his wife die on the operating table. He proceeds to murder them in various ways inspired by the ten curses of Pharaoh. Well done—it inspired a couple of sequels.

THE CAST: Vincent Price, Joseph Cotten, Terry-Thomas, Hugh Griffith, Virginia North

Name that movie!

7. A young couple moves into a mid-Manhattan apartment and discovers that a coven of witches are their neighbors. The husband makes a deal with them to further his career, and as a result his wife bears the devil's child. A potent brew of suspense and terror!

THE CAST: Mia Farrow, John Cassavetes, Ruth Gordon, Sidney Blackmer, Maurice Evans, Ralph Bellamy, Patsy Kelly, Elisha Cook, Jr.

Name that movie!

8. "Possession" is nine-tenths of the law, when you're trying to make a good horror film—and this one was a dilly! Probably the best modern horror film to date.

THE CAST: Linda Blair, Ellen Burstyn, Jason Miller, Jack MacGowran, Max von Sydow

Name that movie!

9. The fine old respected profession of "grave-robbing" pits Boris and Bela against each other. "Man the shovels and picks, boys"—who could ask for anything more! A fine old classic.

THE CAST: Boris Karloff, Bela Lugosi, Henry Daniell, Edith Atwater, Russell Wade, Rita Corday

Name that movie!

10. A hand (nothing else!) is on the loose, seeking revenge for the murder of the pianist it once belonged to. They talk about kids and dogs as "scene stealers," but I'll bet on this "hand" every time!

THE CAST: Peter Lorre, Andrea King, Robert Alda, J. Carrol Naish

Name that movie!

11. Franky gets married! But I shouldn't make light of one of the best Frankenstein films ever made.

THE CAST: Boris Karloff, Colin Clive, Valerie Hobson, Elsa Lanchester, Una O'Connor, E. E. Clive, Dwight Frye

Name that movie!

12. Dana Andrews sets out to investigate a fake devil cult in modern-day England. Much to his dismay, he discovers that this is not a fake cult after all, and a death curse is put on him by the cult's leader. The kind of stuff that good horror films are made of!

THE CAST: Dana Andrews, Niall MacGinnis, Peggy Cummins, Athene Seyler

Name that movie!

13. A mysterious fortune-teller confronts five strangers on a train and predicts all of their deaths in gruesome detail. Well done—a winner! Moral: avoid fortune-tellers with tarot cards on moving trains.

THE CAST: Peter Cushing, Ursula Howells, Max Adrian, Roy Castle, Christopher Lee, Michael Gough, Donald Sutherland, Jeremy Kemp, Kenny Lynch

Name that movie!

14. The original story of the original caped crusader who was always dressed to kill after dark.

THE CAST: Bela Lugosi, Helen Chandler, David Manners, Dwight Frye, Edward Van Sloan, Frances Dade

Name that movie!

15. "Leaping Lizards!" That could have been the title of this flickering flick. It all takes place on a secluded island (Man, those secluded islands are rough!) where Mother Nature goes bananas and the lizard and insect life overrun the place.

THE CAST: Ray Milland, Sam Elliott, Joan Van Ark, Adam Roarke, Judy Pace

Name that movie!

16. A scientist experiments with teleportation (breaking down matter into components, transmitting these bits to another location and reassembling them back into the original matter). Unfortunately, he fails to notice that an insect is in the teleportation booth with him at the time of his experiment. I leave the rest to your imagination. Regrettably, the producers of this film did not!

THE CAST: David Hedison, Vincent Price, Herbert Marshall, Patricia Owens

Name that movie!

17. A classic horror film, it dealt with Egyptology and set it back 4,000 years. (Come to think of it, that's where it was supposed to be in the first place.) A first-class "unraveling" of suspense and terror!

THE CAST: Boris Karloff, Zita Johann, David Manners, Arthur Byron, Edward Van Sloan, Bramwell Fletcher, Noble Johnson

Name that movie!

18. Set in the high-brow world of music, this excellent horror film has had audiences hitting high notes with their screams of fright for over fifty years!

THE CAST: Lon Chaney, Mary Philbin, Norman Kerry, Arthur Edmund Carewe

Name that movie!

19. Now you see him . . . now you don't!

THE CAST: Claude Rains, Gloria Stuart, William Harrigan, Henry Travers, E. E. Clive, Una O'Connor

Name that movie!

20. Five people are lost in some catacombs. They meet a weird monk (Lucifer in disguise) who tells them terrifying tales of the future. A fine cast, and it's absolutely horrific!

THE CAST: Ralph Richardson, Geoffrey Bayldon, Peter Cushing, Joan Collins, Robin Phillips, Richard Greene, Nigel Patrick, Patrick Magee

Name that movie!

True or false?

1. In *Godzilla* (1956) the actor who played the role of the reporter who described the destruction of Tokyo was Raymond Burr (Star of *Perry Mason* and *Ironside*).

2. *The Return of the Vampire* (1943) tells the story of the reappearance of Dracula during the London blitz.

3. The comedy team of Abbott and Costello made films with both Boris Karloff and Bela Lugosi.

4. *I Was a Teenage Werewolf* (1957) starred Michael Landon of *Bonanza* and *Little House on the Prairie* fame.

5. *Trog* (1970) was a flick about a "missing link" alive in the twentieth century and starred Joan Crawford as an anthropologist.

6. *Mighty Joe Young* (1949) was a sequel to *King Kong.*

7. *The Green Slime* (1969) was a remake of *The Blob* (1958).

8. In *The Beast from 20,000 Fathoms* (1953) the creature is finally cornered in the Coney Island amusement park.

9. *The Beginning of the End* (1957) tells the story of a growing army of giant radioactive insects (mainly grasshoppers) who threaten to devour the world.

10. Richard Denning, who plays the role of governor of Hawaii on TV's *Hawaii Five O,* has appeared in a number of horror films during his career.

11. *The Thing with Two Heads* (1972) is the story of a bigoted scientist who saves his own life by having his head transplanted onto the body of a black man.

12. The only movies ever made about King Kong were the original film in 1933 and its remake in 1977.

13. The role of the doctor in *Rosemary's Baby* (1968) was played by Vincent Price.

14. Bette Davis starred with Oliver Reed and Karen Black in the chiller *Burnt Offerings* (1976).

15. Boris Karloff was the only actor who ever portrayed Frankenstein on the screen.

16. *Blood Alley* (1955) was a horror film about the exploits of Dracula in the back streets of London.

17. *The Mummy* (1959) starred Boris Karloff.

18. *House of Wax* (1953) was the first major horror film shot in 3-D (three-dimension process).

19. *Night People* (1954) was a chiller about zombies on the loose and starred Vincent Price.

20. *Flesh Feast* (1970) was a horrible horror film which starred that glamorous gal of the forties, Veronica Lake.

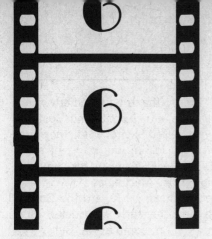

Comedies

Is it true that one's happiest experiences are the best remembered? We're going to test this theory right now as we probe your memories of the comedies.

"Make 'em laugh" has been one of filmdom's traditions right from the start. Chaplin, Laurel and Hardy, the Marx Brothers and many others gave us broad, slapstick comedy that audiences loved. Early on, too, "situation" comedy became a regular bill of fare at movie theaters. The top stars of the day—Gable, Lombard, Colbert, Grant, Dunne, Stewart, Cooper, William Powell, Loy, Tracy, Hepburn—and a host of other stellar names starred regularly in situation comedies.

Then, in the forties and fifties, the broad comedy films evolved into a kind of zany style with Abbott and Costello, Martin and Lewis, Danny Kaye and Red Skelton. Still, the situation comedies were going strong. Joining the ranks of all of the old favorites were people like Rock Husdon, Jack Lemmon, Doris Day, Deborah Kerr and Shirley MacLaine.

Today, in the sophisticated eighties, we regard the Golden Age of Comedy (the silents and the early slapsticks) as a thing of the past—an era that will not come again. But, we've still got the romantic comedies, the domestic comedies, the social comedies, the political comedies—and they are all here to stay! Today's newer light-comedy stars include such names as Warren Beatty, Burt Reynolds, Woody Allen, Robert Redford, George Segal, Ryan O'Neal, Jane Fonda, Glenda Jackson, Barbra Streisand, Jill Clayburgh and Diane Keaton.

Clearly, the Hollywood comedy tradition is still going strong!

Name that star!

1. This popular Hollywood star has built his career by appearing in a long string of comedy films, though he has demonstrated his straight dramatic talents on occasion.

FILM CREDITS: The Apartment *(1960)*
How to Murder Your Wife *(1965)*
The Fortune Cookie *(1966)*
The Odd Couple *(1968)*
The April Fools *(1969)*
The Out-of-Towners *(1969)*

Name that star!

2. This fine British actor has appeared in many dramatic roles, but he also has scored repeatedly in some marvelous droll comedies.

FILM CREDITS: Kind Hearts and Coronets *(1949)*
The Lavender Hill Mob *(1951)*
The Man in the White Suit *(1951)*
The Captain's Paradise *(1952)*
The Ladykillers *(1955)*
A Majority of One *(1961)*

Name that star!

3. This great screen idol has perfected the art of playing romantic comedy leads.

FILM CREDITS: The Talk of the Town *(1942)*
Arsenic and Old Lace *(1944)*
The Bachelor and the Bobbysoxer *(1947)*
I Was a Male War Bride *(1949)*
Monkey Business *(1952)*
That Touch of Mink *(1962)*

Name that star!

4. A very lanky, shy leading man and a fine actor, this fellow used his unique style effectively in some light comedies.

FILM CREDITS: Mr. Deeds Goes to Town *(1936)*
The Cowboy and the Lady *(1939)*
Ball of Fire *(1942)*
Casanova Brown *(1944)*
Along Came Jones *(1945)*
Good Sam *(1948)*

Name that star!

5. She was the queen of romantic comedies in the fifties and sixties.

FILM CREDITS: Please Don't Eat the Daisies *(1960)*
Lover Come Back *(1962)*
That Touch of Mink *(1962)*
The Thrill of It All *(1963)*
Move Over Darling *(1963)*
Send Me No Flowers *(1964)*

Name that star!

6. One of our finest actresses, she has used her talents effectively in many excellent light comedies.

FILM CREDITS: The Philadelphia Story *(1940)*
Woman of the Year *(1942)*
Adam's Rib *(1949)*
Pat and Mike *(1952)*
Desk Set *(1957)*
Guess Who's Coming to Dinner *(1967)*

Name that star!

7. Inventive, zany and often slapstick comedy was this comic's domain. He was quite popular in the fifties and sixties.

FILM CREDITS: The Stooge *(1953)*
The Delicate Delinquent *(1957)*
Visit to a Small Planet *(1960)*
The Bellboy *(1960)*
The Nutty Professor *(1963)*
The Disorderly Orderly *(1964)*

Name that star!

8. He is an excellent sophisticated actor-comedian and perennial friend of the leading man in romantic comedies.

FILM CREDITS: The Mating Game *(1959)*
Pillow Talk *(1959)*
Let's Make Love *(1961)*
Lover Come Back *(1961)*
Boys' Night Out *(1962)*
Send Me No Flowers *(1964)*

Name that star!

9. This Englishman is one of the most talented and clever comic actors in films today.

FILM CREDITS: The Mouse That Roared *(1959)*
The Battle of the Sexes *(1960)*
A Shot in the Dark *(1964)*
What's New Pussycat? *(1965)*
I Love You Alice B. Toklas *(1968)*
There's a Girl in My Soup *(1970)*

Name that star!

10. For years and years he's been America's top comedian. His funny radio-style dialogue and asides to the audience are his trademarks in films.

FILM CREDITS: Caught in the Draft *(1941)*
My Favorite Blonde *(1942)*
They Got Me Covered *(1942)*
Monsieur Beaucaire *(1946)*
Sorrowful Jones *(1948)*
Boy Did I Get a Wrong Number *(1956)*

Name that star!

11. She was a beautiful brash blonde who was quite at home in light romantic comedies.

FILM CREDITS: Twentieth Century *(1934)*
Hands across the Table *(1935)*
My Man Godfrey *(1936)*
True Confession *(1937)*
Nothing Sacred *(1937)*
Mr. and Mrs. Smith *(1941)*
To Be or Not To Be *(1942)*

Name that star!

12. This appealing actress was quite popular in romantic comedies of the thirties and forties. She always managed to play smart and rather liberated women.

FILM CREDITS: It Happened One Night *(1934)*
Skylark *(1941)*
Practically Yours *(1945)*
Without Reservations *(1946)*
The Egg and I *(1947)*
Bride for Sale *(1947)*

Name that star!

13. This glib, talented comic actress usually played career women in light comedies.

FILM CREDITS: His Girl Friday *(1940)*
No Time for Comedy *(1940)*
Hired Wife *(1940)*
The Feminine Touch *(1941)*
My Sister Eileen *(1942)*
Auntie Mame *(1958)*

Name that star!

14. This pert little blond—with a squeaky but cute sort of voice—was very popular in the thirties and forties. She always seemed to be cast as the heroine in social-minded romantic comedies.

FILM CREDITS: Mr. Deeds Goes to Town *(1936)*
You Can't Take It with You *(1938)*
Mr. Smith Goes to Washington *(1939)*
The Devil and Miss Jones *(1941)*
The Talk of the Town *(1942)*
The More the Merrier *(1943)*

Name that star!

15. Although she is remembered as a dancer-actress, this star had a fine flair for light comedy.

FILM CREDITS: The Gay Divorcee *(1934)*
Bachelor Mother *(1939)*
Lucky Partners *(1940)*
The Major and the Minor *(1943)*
Monkey Business *(1952)*
Oh Men, Oh Women *(1957)*

Name that star!

16. This American character actor was usually seen on the screen with a cigar and wearing a monocle. He played crusty types—businessmen, fathers and rich uncles. He certainly performed yeoman's service as a supporting actor in many delightful comedies.

FILM CREDITS: The Lady Eve *(1941)*
The Devil and Miss Jones *(1941)*
Yes Sir, That's My Baby *(1949)*
Monkey Business *(1952)*
How to Murder a Rich Uncle *(1957)*
The Remarkable Mr. Pennypacker *(1959)*

Name that star!

17. This suave, versatile British leading man established himself in Hollywood. He has had a long, durable career that has encompassed a score of romantic comedies.

FILM CREDITS: The Bishop's Wife *(1947)*
The Moon Is Blue *(1953)*
Oh Men, Oh Women *(1957)*
Please Don't Eat the Daisies *(1960)*
The Pink Panther *(1964)*
Prudence and the Pill *(1968)*

Name that star!

18. This lady was a popular actress during the thirties and forties. Aside from the *Thin Man* series of films, domestic comedies were her forte.

FILM CREDITS: The Thin Man *(1934)*
Double Wedding *(1937)*
Love Crazy *(1941)*
The Bachelor and the Bobbysoxer *(1947)*
Mr. Blandings Builds His Dream House *(1948)*
Cheaper by the Dozen *(1950)*

Name that star!

19. This tall, thin, likeable actor is one of Hollywood's greats. His long and varied career has included some very memorable light comedies.

FILM CREDITS: You Can't Take It with You *(1938)*
It's a Wonderful World *(1939)*
Mr. Smith Goes to Washington *(1939)*
No Time for Comedy *(1940)*
The Philadelphia Story *(1940)*
Harvey *(1950)*

Name that star!

20. One of America's top radio comedians, he moved on to TV with great success. He also managed to retain his stingy, self-centered character pose.

FILM CREDITS: Charlie's Aunt *(1941)*
To Be or Not to Be *(1942)*
George Washington Slept Here *(1942)*
It's in the Bag *(1945)*
The Horn Blows at Midnight *(1945)*

Name that star!

Rosalind Russell, Cary Grant and
Billy Gilbert in *His Girl Friday* (1940).

The Marx Brothers (Groucho, Chico and Harpo)
and Allan Jones in *A Night at the Opera* (1935).

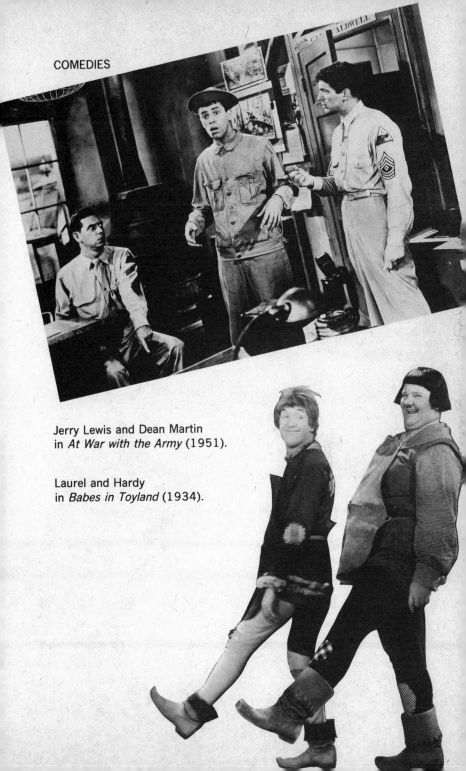

Jerry Lewis and Dean Martin
in *At War with the Army* (1951).

Laurel and Hardy
in *Babes in Toyland* (1934).

ROMANCE-
MELODRAMA

Clark Gable and Joan Crawford
in *Strange Cargo* (1940).

Gary Cooper and Barbara Stanwyck
in *Meet John Doe* (1941).

Laurence Olivier
and Merle Oberon
in the classic
Wuthering Heights (1939).

Robert Taylor
and Greta Garbo
in *Camille* (1937).

Raymond Massey pointing to the stars
in the classic *Things to Come* (1936).

Destination Moon (1950).

Robbie the Robot, Leslie Nielsen, Walter Pidgeon and Anne Francis in *Forbidden Planet* (1956).

Grant Williams and hungry friend in *The Incredible Shrinking Man* (1957).

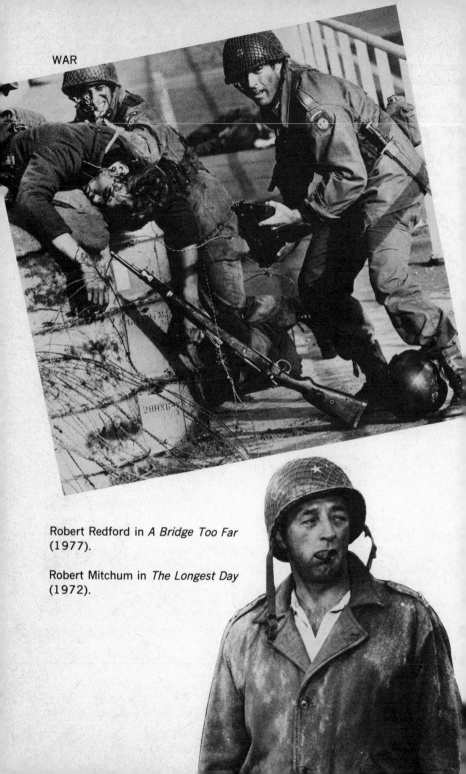

Robert Redford in *A Bridge Too Far* (1977).

Robert Mitchum in *The Longest Day* (1972).

Dana Andrews in
A Walk in the Sun (1946).

Tyrone Power and
Betty Grable in
A Yank in the R.A.F.
(1941).

Name that star!

Multiple choice

1. Back in the fifites, there was a series of movies about Francis, the talking mule. Mickey Rooney starred in the seventh and last film, but who starred in the other six?
a. Eddie Bracken b. Donald O'Connor c. Eddie Albert
d. Danny Kaye e. Red Skelton

2. Who played the title role in *Gidget* (1959), which was a teen-age, beach-locale comedy?
a. Sandra Dee b. Debbie Reynolds c. Ann-Margret
d. Sally Field e. Shirley Temple

3. Who was the beautiful blonde (with a beauty mark on her cheek) who starred with the Marx Brothers in *Love Happy* (1949)?
a. Signe Hasso b. Ginger Rogers c. Ilona Massey d. Zsa Zsa Gabor e. Virginia Mayo

4. Bob Hope's co-star in *Sorrowful Jones* (1948) and *Fancy Pants* (1950) was_____?
a. Loretta Young b. Maureen O'Hara c. Betty Hutton
d. Paulette Goddard e. Lucille Ball

5. Who played the lead in *The Fuller Brush Man* (1948)?
a. Donald O'Connor b. Red Skelton c. Danny Kaye
d. Eddie Bracken e. Mickey Rooney

6. Who starred in *The Fuller Brush Girl* (1950)?
a. Ginger Rogers b. Patsy Kelly c. Lucille Ball d. Doris Day e. Betty Hutton

7. *I Married a Witch* (1942) was the basis for the TV series *Bewitched*. The film starred Fredric March, but who played the witch?
a. Elizabeth Montgomery b. Veronica Lake c. Ava Gardner d. Lizabeth Scott e. Irene Dunne

8. Who was the star of *The Human Comedy* (1943)?
a. Gary Cooper   **b.** James Stewart   **c.** Gene Kelly
d. Henry Fonda   **e.** Danny Kaye

9. Who starred with Debbie Reynolds in *The Tender Trap* (1955)?
a. Van Johnson   **b.** Donald O'Connor   **c.** Gene Kelly
d. Frank Sinatra   **e.** Rock Hudson

10. The Neil Simon comedy *Barefoot in the Park* was made into a movie in 1967. It starred Jane Fonda. Who co-starred?
a. Jack Lemmon   **b.** Paul Newman   **c.** Robert Redford
d. Walter Matthau   **e.** James Garner

11. *The Moon Is Blue* (1953) starred two of Hollywood's popular leading men. One was David Niven. Who was the other?
a. Glenn Ford   **b.** Gregory Peck   **c.** Gary Cooper   **d.** James Stewart   **e.** William Holden

12. Name the popular actress who starred with George Peppard in *Breakfast at Tiffany's* (1961).
a. Audrey Hepburn   **b.** Eleanor Parker   **c.** Deborah Kerr
d. Ann Blyth   **e.** Sophia Loren

13. The comedy *The Russians Are Coming, the Russians Are Coming* (1966) starred a famous TV comic. What was his name?
a. Tim Conway   **b.** Jackie Gleason   **c.** Sid Caesar   **d.** Carl Reiner   **e.** George Gobel

14. In the *Topper* comedy series of films, a strait-laced banker is haunted and helped by the ghosts of his friends, the Kirbys, whom only he can see. Who played the role of Mr. Topper, the banker?
a. Adolphe Menjou   **b.** Roland Young   **c.** Gene Lockhart
d. Walter Abel   **e.** Charles Winninger

15. Who starred in *The Magnificent Dope* (1942)?
a. Henry Fonda   **b.** Red Skelton   **c.** Fred MacMurray
d. Jack Carson   **e.** Ralph Bellamy

16. Who starred with Barbra Streisand in *What's Up Doc* (1972)?
a. George Segal   **b.** Robert Redford   **c.** Ryan O'Neal
d. Woody Allen   **e.** Warren Beatty

17. Who starred with Woody Allen in *Bananas* (1971)?
a. Janet Margolin   **b.** Louise Lasser   **c.** Diane Keaton
d. Susan Anspach   **e.** Shelley Winters

18. Who played the lead in that hilarious comedy *The Man Who Came to Dinner* (1941)?
a. Spencer Tracy   **b.** Clifton Webb   **c.** Charles Coburn
d. Charles Laughton   **e.** Monty Woolley

19. *The Miracle of Morgan's Creek* (1944) starred _____?
a. Jane Wyman   **b.** Betty Grable   **c.** Betty Hutton
d. Lucille Ball   **e.** Jean Arthur

20. In that classic Christmas comedy *Miracle on 34th Street* (1947), who starred as Santa Claus?
a. Charlie Ruggles   **b.** John McGiver   **c.** Edmund Gwenn
d. Edward Arnold   **e.** Cecil Kellaway

21. Who co-starred in the Doris Day comedy *The Glass Bottom Boat* (1966)?
a. Rod Taylor   **b.** David Niven   **c.** James Garner   **d.** Rock Hudson   **e.** Richard Widmark

22. Who starred with Danny Kaye in *The Secret Life of Walter Mitty* (1947)?
a. Virginia Mayo   **b.** Jane Russell   **c.** Ann Sheridan
d. Myrna Loy   **e.** Doris Day

23. In *The Hot Rock* (1972), a comedy about a diamond caper, who starred along with George Segal?
a. Robert Redford   **b.** Alan Arkin   **c.** Paul Newman
d. Robert Wagner   **e.** Donald Sutherland

24. The weird goings-on in a city hospital were the subject of a terrific black comedy, *The Hospital* (1971). Who starred in it?
a. Alan Alda   **b.** Donald Sutherland   **c.** Burt Reynolds
d. George C. Scott   **e.** James Coburn

25. In *Bunny O'Hare* (1971), a middle-aged widow and an ex-con become bank robbers disguised as hippies. They make their getaway on a motorcycle. Who starred in this comedy clinker along with Ernest Borgnine?
a. Anne Bancroft   **b.** Bette Davis   **c.** Ingrid Bergman
d. Lucille Ball   **e.** Elizabeth Taylor

26. Who starred in the 1968 comedy, *Buona Sera, Mrs. Campbell?*
a. Sophia Loren   **b.** Virna Lisi   **c.** Gina
Lollobrigida   **d.** Shirley MacLaine   **e.** Leslie Caron

27. Who starred in *The Catered Affair* (1956)?
a. Bette Davis   **b.** Joan Fontaine   **c.** Greer
Garson   **d.** Celeste Holm   **e.** Olivia De Havilland

28. *Catch-22* (1970), a black comedy about World War II, starred _____?
a. Alan Alda   **b.** Alan Arkin   **c.** Robert Mitchum
d. David Niven   **e.** Robert Morse

29. Who starred in *Cheaper by the Dozen* (1950)?
a. William Powell   **b.** Clifton Webb   **c.** Brian Keith
d. Walter Pidgeon   **e.** Tony Randall

30. Who starred with Clark Gable in *Comrade X* (1940)?
a. Donna Reed   **b.** Hedy Lamarr   **c.** Lana Turner   **d.** Claire Trevor   **e.** Carole Lombard

31. The hillbilly comedy films about *Ma and Pa Kettle* began in 1949 and ran until 1956. Who starred as Ma Kettle?
a. Patsy Kelly   **b.** Joan Davis   **c.** Fay Bainter   **d.** Marjorie Main   **e.** Ethel Barrymore

32. The 1972 comedy *Pete 'n' Tillie* starred Walter Matthau as Pete. Who starred as Tillie?
a. Carol Burnett   **b.** Sandy Dennis   **c.** Louise Fletcher
d. Celeste Holm   **e.** Goldie Hawn

33. The 1969 film version of the hit comedy *Cactus Flower* starred Walter Matthau. Who co-starred?
a. Rosalind Russell   **b.** Ingrid Bergman   **c.** Angela Lansbury   **d.** Deborah Kerr   **e.** Alexis Smith

34. In the *Blondie* comedy film series, which was based on the comic strip still popular today, who starred as Dagwood Bumstead?
a. William Bendix   **b.** Donald O'Connor   **c.** Arthur Lake
d. Joe E. Brown   **e.** Frank McHugh

35. Who was the noted film comedian who played the nervous little bald-headed, hen-pecked husband in many films? He also played the role of Knobby Walsh, Joe Palooka's manager, in the film series based on that comic strip.
a. Guy Kibbee   **b.** Charles Winninger   **c.** Leon Errol
d. Charlie Ruggles   **e.** S. Z. Sakall

36. Who starred as the bumbling Chester A. Riley in *The Life of Riley* (1949)?
a. Jackie Gleason   **b.** Danny Kaye   **c.** William Bendix
d. Eddie Bracken   **e.** Aldo Ray

37. Who was the actress who starred in *Our Miss Brooks* (1956) after starring in the TV series based on that character?
a. Nanette Fabray **b.** Eve Arden **c.** Donna Reed
d. Nancy Walker **e.** Shirley Jones

38. Who was the famous tough-guy comedian who starred in the thirties and forties in such memorable films as *Min and Bill* (1930), *Tugboat Annie* (1933), *Barnacle Bill* (1941), *Barbary Coast Gent* (1944) and *The Mighty McGuirk* (1947)?
a. Spencer Tracy **b.** Victor McLaglen **c.** Pat O'Brien
d. William Demarest **e.** Wallace Beery

39. Who starred with the great W. C. Fields in *My Little Chickadee* (1940)?
a. Carole Lombard **b.** Greta Garbo **c.** Mae West
d. Gracie Fields **e.** Janet Gaynor

40. *Sons of the Desert* (1933), a comedy classic, starred which of these great comedy teams?
a. The Marx Brothers **b.** The Ritz Brothers **c.** Martin and Lewis **d.** Laurel and Hardy **e.** Abbott and Costello

Name that movie!

1. An angel is sent down to Earth on a terrible mission. At an appointed hour, he is to blow Gabriel's horn and thus cause the destruction of the entire world. Benny and the cast are great and the film is a comedy gem!

THE CAST: Jack Benny, Alexis Smith, Dolores Moran, Allyn Joslyn, Guy Kibbee, Reginald Gardiner, Franklin Pangborn, John Alexander, Margaret Dumont

Name that movie!

2. A chimp in a research lab accidently concocts a solution that instantly restores "youth." Picture Cary Grant behaving like a two-year-old. An excellent cast makes the most of a wild, thin premise.

THE CAST: Cary Grant, Ginger Rogers, Charles Coburn, Marilyn Monroe, Hugh Marlowe

Name that movie!

3. A genius who knows "everything" has a grudge against a soap company. He goes on their weekly radio quiz show and begins to win huge sums of money. The soap company panics and tries to foil him. Top satirical entertainment and still timely.

THE CAST: Ronald Colman, Vincent Price, Celeste Holm, Barbara Britton, Art Linkletter

Name that movie!

4. A crack lady newspaper reporter wants to quit her job and get married. Her editor tricks her into handling just one more big story in an attempt to foil her personal plans. It's a marvelous comedy riot; everyone involved is at the top of their form—a classic!

THE CAST: Rosalind Russell, Cary Grant, Ralph Bellamy, Gene Lockhart, Porter Hall, Ernest Truex, Cliff Edwards, Frank Orth, John Qualen, Roscoe Karns, Frank Jenks, Clarence Kolb, Abner Biberman, Billy Gilbert, Marion Martin, Alma Kluger

Name that movie!

5. A super Keystone-cops style comedy. An assorted group of people learn of some buried loot and try to outrace each other to find it. It's a major assault on the eye, ear and funnybone—memorable madness.

THE CAST: Spencer Tracy, Jimmy Durante, Milton Berle, Sid Caesar, Ethel Merman, Buddy Hackett, Mickey Rooney, Dick Shawn, Phil Silvers, Terry-Thomas, Jonathan Winters, Edie Adams, Dorothy Provine, Eddie Anderson, plus many guest stars

Name that movie!

6. An asthmatic lawyer ducks out on his domineering fiancée and nagging mother. He joins the flower people and whiffs the weed. There are some great moments in this mild satirical farce, and Sellers is almost always worth watching.

THE CAST: Peter Sellers, Jo Van Fleet, Joyce Van Patten, Leigh Taylor-Young, David Arkin, Herb Edelman

Name that movie!

7. An office worker rents out his midtown pad to company executives as an after-hours playpen. He learns that one of these guys is after his girl. A humorous slice of city life.

THE CAST: Jack Lemmon, Shirley MacLaine, Fred MacMurray, Ray Walston, Jack Kruschen, Edie Adams, David Lewis

Name that movie!

8. Two sweet old sisters, their mad brother and a homicidal nephew rack up an impressive body count in their Brooklyn home. A black farce which only goes to prove that murder can be funny—very funny!

THE CAST: Cary Grant, Josephine Hull, Jean Adair, Raymond Massey, Peter Lorre, Priscilla Lane, Edward Everett Horton, James Gleason, John Alexander, Jack Carson, Grant Mitchell

Name that movie!

9. A penniless member of a wealthy English family doggedly (and comically) proceeds to murder the eight other relatives who stand between him and the family fortune. An excellent English comedy—witty, stylish and hilarious!

THE CAST: Dennis Price, Alec Guinness, Valerie Hobson, Joan Greenwood

Name that movie!

10. A fly-by-night Broadway producer seduces wealthy old ladies into investing in a play. He sells the total interest in this production many times over because he's sure it will be a flop and he won't have to return any of the money. His scheme backfires when this horrible play becomes an overnight smash. Wildly funny—it's a classic!

THE CAST: Zero Mostel, Gene Wilder, Kenneth Mars, Estelle Winwood, Renee Taylor, Dick Shawn

Name that movie!

11. A comic-strip cartoonist and confirmed bachelor marries. He expresses his marital frustrations and the desire to get rid of his wife in his comic-strip story. When his wife disappears he is tried for murder. Humorous, but disappointing.

THE CAST: Jack Lemmon, Virna Lisi, Terry-Thomas, Eddie Mayehoff, Sidney Blackmer, Claire Trevor

Name that movie!

12. A lawyer, who is some shrewd cookie, pushes his client into faking a severe injury from an accident and suing for a million dollars. Good premise, but a talented team (Lemmon and Matthau) suffer from script whiplash.

THE CAST: Walter Matthau, Jack Lemmon, Ron Rich, Cliff Osmond, Lurene Tuttle, Judi West

Name that movie!

13. A quiet married man finds it's that time in his life when he must have a fling. He attempts an affair with his beautiful upstairs neighbor. This film version of a successful Broadway comedy scratches out a lot of laughs for itself.

THE CAST: Tom Ewell, Marilyn Monroe, Sonny Tufts, Evelyn Keyes, Robert Strauss, Oscar Homolka, Marguerite Chapman, Victor Moore

Name that movie!

14. An "enchanting" comedy about a publisher who discovers that his new girl friend is really a witch. This film version of a successful Broadway show makes for an amusing brew.

THE CAST: James Stewart, Kim Novak, Jack Lemmon, Ernie Kovacs, Hermione Gingold, Elsa Lanchester, Janice Rule

Name that movie!

15. The bumbling Inspector Clouseau was introduced to audiences in this film. He is in Switzerland on the trail of a notorious jewel thief known as The Phantom. Sellers is marvelous—broad, slapstick comedy in high gear!

THE CAST: David Niven, Peter Sellers, Capucine, Claudia Cardinale, Robert Wagner

Name that movie!

16. A comical "mob" of characters are led by a timid bank clerk who plans and executes a daring bullion robbery in England. The characters and details are marvelously conceived. This is the funniest band of crooks ever seen on the screen—a comedy masterpiece!

THE CAST: Alec Guinness, Stanley Holloway, Sidney James, Alfie Bass, Marjorie Fielding, Edie Martin, John Gregson, Gibb MacLaughlin

Name that movie!

17. A wife has just been rescued from a five-year shipwrecked stay on a desert island. She returns home to find that her husband has just remarried. A cast of pros at work, and if you love Doris, you love the whole thing.

THE CAST: Doris Day, James Garner, Polly Bergen, Thelma Ritter, Chuck Connors, Fred Clark

Name that movie!

18. The dumb blonde mistress of a tough, self-made businessman wants to improve herself, culturally speaking. She falls for her English tutor and manages to outwit her lover. A Broadway hit that gives "birth" (that's a clue) to a fine comedy film.

THE CAST: Judy Holliday, Broderick Crawford, William Holden, Howard St. John

Name that movie!

19. "Marxism" is the most delightful brand of zany comedy to ever hit the big screen. In this superb episode, the boys help a gal who owns a sanatorium and a racehorse. Side-splitting!

THE CAST: Groucho, Chico, Harpo, Margaret Dumont, Maureen O'Sullivan, Allan Jones, Douglass Dumbrille, Esther Muir, Sig Rumann

Name that movie!

20. A sophisticated "rib-tickler" with top performances from Tracy and Hepburn as husband and wife lawyers on opposite sides of a trial for attempted murder.

THE CAST: Spencer Tracy, Katharine Hepburn, David Wayne, Tom Ewell, Judy Holliday, Jean Hagen

Name that movie!

True or false?

1. Bob Hope and Bing Crosby made a number of "Road" pictures together—*Road to Singapore* (1940), *Road to Zanzibar* (1941), *Road to Morocco* (1942), *Road to Utopia* (1945), *Road to Rio* (1947), *Road to Bali* (1952)—and Dorothy Lamour co-starred with them in all of these films.

2. Groucho Marx never appeared in a film without Harpo and Chico.

3. The only film in which comedian Milton Berle ever appeared in was *It's a Mad, Mad, Mad, Mad World* (1963).

4. The comedy team of Abbott and Costello without exception appeared in films together.

5. Leo Gorcey was the leader of the Bowery Boys.

6. The famous radio comedian Fred Allen never made a movie.

7. The American comic actor who was very popular in the forties and starred in *The Miracle of Morgan's Creek* (1943) and *Hail the Conquering Hero* (1944) was Eddie Bracken.

8. Hedy Lamarr and Marlene Dietrich were James Stewart's leading ladies at some time in his film career.

9. Jackie Cooper played Henry Aldrich in the first two films of the *Henry Aldrich* series.

10. Jimmy Durante was one of the stars of the sophisticated comedy *The Man Who Came to Dinner* (1941).

11. The child actor who appeared in *Our Gang* shorts, *The Champ* (1931) and *Treasure Island* (1934) was Jackie Cooper.

12. Blake Edwards was the writer-director of many comedy films, including *The Pink Panther* (1963).

13. The comic character actor who usually played a fat, excitable Italian and who was a stooge for Laurel and Hardy, the Three Stooges and the Marx Brothers was Billy De Wolfe.

14. The rugged, cheerful and comical actor who appeared in many action films, including *The Adventures of Robin Hood* (1938) as Little John, was Alan Hale.

15. *The Great Dictator* (1940) starred Charlie Chaplin and was a "sound" production.

16. *Guess Who's Coming to Dinner* (1967) was a remake of *The Man Who Came to Dinner* (1941).

17. *Heaven Can Wait* (1979) was a remake of *Heaven Can Wait* (1943).

18. The Disney Studio comedy, *The Absent-Minded Professor* (1961) starred Fred MacMurray.

19. The American actor who usually played comically befuddled but lovable characters, including the title role in *The Wizard of Oz* (1939), was Frank Morgan.

20. The star of *The Buster Keaton Story* (1957) was Red Skelton.

Romance-
Melodrama

Long before the advent of TV soap operas, radio and Hollywood film studios were in the business of producing "soaps." How many times have you sat in the dark of the movie theater and overheard something like this: "Pass the popcorn, Mary." "Don't bother me now, John, I'm trying to find another hanky."

The fantastic success of the classic *Gone With the Wind* assured us that film makers would continue to make "romance-melodrama" their main film production category indefinitely.

A list of the great novels and plays that have been made into films would run for pages and pages and would include

Rebecca, Jane Eyre, The Magnificent Ambersons, Pride and Prejudice, Forever Amber, A Streetcar Named Desire and *Peyton Place.* Looking back at any year in the history of film making, you can easily find a dozen or so big romance-melo-drama productions—always starring the top names in the business.

Despite the TV soap operas, good romance-melodramas (recently *The Way We Were* and *Love Story*) always make big money at the box office. No one can really compete with Hollywood; they've got the big screen and the big stars to create that larger-than-life illusion that audiences love. Now, let's recall some of the most melodramatic moments ever shown on the big screen.

Name that star!

1. He was an international film star and played a wide variety of roles. However, he came to be regarded as the screen's "great lover."

FILM CREDITS: History Is Made at Night *(1937)*
All This and Heaven Too *(1940)*
Hold Back the Dawn *(1941)*
The Constant Nymph *(1943)*
Cluny Brown *(1946)*
Fanny *(1962)*

Name that star!

2. This actress was a popular international star in the forties and fifties.

FILM CREDITS: Intermezzo *(1939)*
Rage in Heaven *(1941)*
Casablanca *(1943)*
For Whom the Bell Tolls *(1943)*
Saratoga Trunk *(1945)*
Notorious *(1946)*

Name that star!

3. One of Hollywood's top stars, this suave leading man is best known for his work in romantic comedies and melodramas.

FILM CREDITS: Penny Serenade *(1941)*
Once Upon a Honeymoon *(1942)*
Notorious *(1946)*
An Affair to Remember *(1957)*
Indiscreet *(1958)*
Houseboat *(1958)*

Name that star!

4. A charming American leading lady of the thirties and forties, she always played sensible, nice girls and had much success in romantic comedies and melodramas.

FILM CREDITS: Magnificent Obsession *(1935)*
Love Affair *(1939)*
Penny Serenade *(1941)*
Anna and the King of Siam *(1946)*

Name that star!

5. One of Hollywood's most popular and enduring leading ladies, she always starred in romantic melodramas. She usually played a wealthy, high-bred woman suffering the slings and arrows of outrageous fortune.

FILM CREDITS: Mildred Pierce *(1945)*
Humoresque *(1946)*
Possessed *(1947)*
Daisy Kenyon *(1947)*
Harriet Craig *(1950)*
Autumn Leaves *(1956)*

Name that star!

6. This leading lady often played shy, high-born women. Later in her career, she played sophisticated society types.

FILM CREDITS: Rebecca *(1940)*
Suspicion *(1941)*
This Above All *(1942)*
The Constant Nymph *(1943)*
Jane Eyre *(1944)*
Letter from an Unknown Woman *(1948)*

Name that star!

7. He was one of America's finest screen actors and a major star for more than thirty years. He always played a tough, straight-talking, level-headed guy with a sense of humor.

FILM CREDITS: San Francisco *(1936)*
Edward My Son *(1949)*
The Mountain *(1956)*
The Last Hurrah *(1958)*
Inherit the Wind *(1960)*

Name that star!

8. She was a top star in the forties, and her distinguished film career spans more than forty years. She tended to play highly dramatic, outspoken and often bitchy women.

FILM CREDITS: Dark Victory *(1939)*
All This and Heaven Too *(1940)*
The Letter *(1940)*
The Little Foxes *(1941)*
Now Voyager *(1942)*
A Stolen Life *(1946)*

Name that star!

9. This distinguished British actor was suave and handsome. He had a sensitive, intelligent style that made him the classiest leading man of his day.

FILM CREDITS: Arrowsmith *(1931)*
The Light that Failed *(1939)*
The Talk of the Town *(1942)*
Random Harvest *(1942)*
Kismet *(1944)*
A Double Life *(1947)*

Name that star!

10. He is a popular British leading man who is quite debonair and has a talent for romantic comedy roles.

FILM CREDITS: The Rake's Progress *(1946)*
Anna and the King of Siam *(1946)*
The Ghost and Mrs. Muir *(1947)*
The Foxes of Harrow *(1947)*

Name that star!

11. One of Hollywood's most popular leading men in the fifties and sixties, he has been most successful in light romantic comedies.

FILM CREDITS: Magnificent Obsession *(1954)*
All That Heaven Allows *(1955)*
Giant *(1956)*
Written on the Wind *(1956)*
A Farewell to Arms *(1957)*
The Spiral Road *(1962)*

Name that star!

12. One of our most talented actresses, she can excel in drama or comedy. She has always managed to play gutsy, determined, intelligent and independent women.

FILM CREDITS: Little Women *(1933)*
Woman of the Year *(1942)*
Dragon Seed *(1944)*
The Rainmaker *(1956)*
Long Day's Journey into Night *(1961)*
The Madwoman of Chaillot *(1969)*

Name that star!

13. She began in films as a child star and went on to become one of the screen's most glamorous personalities in the fifties and sixties.

FILM CREDITS: Raintree County *(1958)*
Cat on a Hot Tin Roof *(1958)*
Butterfield 8 *(1960)*
The VIPs *(1963)*
The Sandpiper *(1965)*
Who's Afraid of Virginia Woolf? *(1966)*

Name that star!

14. A versatile performer—actress, dancer and comedienne—she was extremely popular in romantic comedies and musicals of the thirties and forties.

FILM CREDITS: Kitty Foyle *(1940)*
Weekend at the Waldorf *(1945)*
Oh Men, Oh Women *(1957)*

Name that star!

15. He is one of Hollywood's most popular and durable leading men. His career began in the early forties and continues strong today.

FILM CREDITS: The Valley of Decision *(1944)*
The Great Sinner *(1949)*
Roman Holiday *(1953)*
The Man in the Grey Flannel Suit *(1955)*
Designing Woman *(1957)*
Beloved Infidel *(1959)*

Name that star!

16. A popular leading lady of the forties, she always played gentle, sympathic roles.

FILM CREDITS: The Enchanted Cottage *(1944)*
Till the End of Time *(1946)*
Three Coins in the Fountain *(1954)*
Friendly Persuasion *(1956)*
A Summer Place *(1959)*
The Swiss Family Robinson *(1960)*

Name that star!

17. This handsome blond performer has had a long career as one of Hollywood's most popular leading men.

FILM CREDITS: Rachel and the Stranger *(1948)*
The Country Girl *(1954)*
Love Is a Many-Splendored Thing *(1955)*
Picnic *(1955)*

Name that star!

18. This popular leading lady of the forties and fifties was considered to be one of the world's most beautiful women.

FILM CREDITS: One Touch of Venus *(1948)*
The Barefoot Contessa *(1954)*
Bhowani Junction *(1956)*
The Sun Also Rises *(1957)*
On the Beach *(1959)*
The Night of the Iguana *(1964)*

Name that star!

19. This famous Hollywood star who started out as the "girl next door" type became one of the glamour queens of the forties and fifties.

FILM CREDITS: Cass Timberlane *(1947)*
The Bad and the Beautiful *(1952)*
Peyton Place *(1957)*
Portrait in Black *(1960)*
By Love Possessed *(1961)*
Madame X *(1965)*

Name that star!

20. She became a glamorous leading lady in the forties and usually played sultry types.

FILM CREDITS: The Lady in Question *(1940)*
Blood and Sand *(1941)*
The Lady from Shanghai *(1948)*
The Loves of Carmen *(1948)*
Affair in Trinidad *(1952)*
Separate Tables *(1958)*

Name that star!

Name that star!

Multiple choice

1. *Homecoming* (1948) starred Lana Turner. Who was her co-star?
a. Ray Milland   **b.** Clark Gable   **c.** Robert Taylor
d. Joseph Cotten   **e.** Brian Aherne

2. *Blume in Love* (1973) was an offbeat romance-comedy. Who starred?
a. Jack Lemmon   **b.** Ryan O'Neal   **c.** George Segal
d. Donald Sutherland   **e.** Elliott Gould

3. Who co-starred with Olivia De Havilland in *The Heiress* (1949)?
a. Laurence Olivier   **b.** Marlon Brando   **c.** Orson Welles
d. Montgomery Clift   **e.** David Niven

4. Who played the role of Efrem Zimbalist, Jr.'s mentally disturbed wife in *Home Before Dark* (1958)?
a. Carroll Baker   **b.** Susan Hayward   **c.** Lee Remick
d. Joan Crawford   **e.** Jean Simmons

5. *King's Row* (1941), a terrific Peyton Place type of melodrama, starred Robert Cummings and Ronald Reagan. Who was their co-star?
a. Ann Sheridan   **b.** Bette Davis   **c.** Claire Trevor   **d.** Irene Dunne   **e.** Priscilla Lane

6. Who starred with Clark Gable in the comedy-drama *Forsaking All Others* (1934)?
a. Claudette Colbert   **b.** Carole Lombard   **c.** Joan Crawford   **d.** Jane Wyman   **e.** Jean Arthur

7. *Jane Eyre* (1944) starred Orson Welles and _____?
a. Olivia De Havilland   **b.** Joan Fontaine   **c.** Gene Tierney
d. Myrna Loy   **e.** Greer Garson

8. Claudette Colbert starred in the original *Imitation of Life* (1934), but who starred in the 1959 remake?
a. Susan Hayward   **b.** Linda Darnell   **c.** Lauren Bacall
d. Lana Turner   **e.** Ann Blyth

9. One of the biggest box office winners of all time, *Gone With the Wind* (1939), starred Clark Gable and Vivien Leigh. Who also starred with them in this film?
a. Joan Fontaine   **b.** Bette Davis   **c.** Loretta Young
d. Joan Bennett   **e.** Olivia De Havilland

10. Who starred with Laurence Olivier in *Rebecca* (1940)?
a. Ida Lupino   **b.** Merle Oberon   **c.** Dorothy McGuire
d. Joan Fontaine   **e.** Elizabeth Taylor

11. Who was Elizabeth Taylor's leading man in *A Place in the Sun* (1951)?
a. Gregory Peck   **b.** Charlton Heston   **c.** Montgomery Clift
d. Rock Hudson   **e.** Kirk Douglas

12. *From This Day Forward* (1946) was based on a novel by Garson Kanin. Who starred?
a. Joan Fontaine   **b.** Hedy Lamarr   **c.** Martha Scott
d. Ginger Rogers   **e.** Greer Garson

13. *Female on the Beach* (1955) told the story of a wealthy widow who falls for the guy at the beach house next door. Who played the widow?
a. Lizabeth Scott   **b.** Jane Russell   **c.** Joan Crawford
d. Lana Turner   **e.** Lauren Bacall

14. Who played the lady convict out on parole for Christmas in *I'll Be Seeing You* (1944)?
a. Claire Trevor   **b.** Anne Baxter   **c.** Bette Davis   **d.** Miriam Hopkins   **e.** Ginger Rogers

15. Name the actress who starred in *Peyton Place* (1957).
a. Elizabeth Taylor   **b.** Barbara Stanwyck   **c.** Alexis Smith
d. Dorothy Malone   **e.** Lana Turner

16. Who co-starred with Natalie Wood in *This Property Is Condemned* (1966)?
a. Robert Wagner   **b.** Jeff Chandler   **c.** Robert Redford
d. Van Johnson   **e.** Tony Curtis

17. Eugene O'Neil's classic play *Strange Interlude* came to the screen in 1932. Who co-starred in this film with Clark Gable?
a. Carole Lombard   **b.** Norma Shearer   **c.** Jean Harlow
d. Mary Astor   **e.** Greta Garbo

18. Who played the role of the American spinster in *Summertime* (1955) and co-starred with Rossano Brazzi?
a. Barbara Stanwyck   **b.** Dorothy McGuire   **c.** Katharine Hepburn   **d.** Loretta Young   **e.** Sophia Loren

19. The glamorous actress who starred with Jose Ferrer in *Moulin Rouge* (1952) was _____?
a. Rita Hayworth   **b.** Lana Turner   **c.** Veronica Lake
d. Eva Gabor   **e.** Zsa Zsa Gabor

20. Who was Laurence Olivier's leading lady in *Pride and Prejudice* (1940)?
a. Vivien Leigh   **b.** Jean Arthur   **c.** Greer Garson   **d.** Merle Oberon   **e.** Gene Tierney

21. Who starred with Jane Wyman in *Miracle in the Rain* (1954)?
a. Van Johnson   **b.** Rock Hudson   **c.** James Stewart
d. William Holden   **e.** Glenn Ford

22. Who played Eve, a woman with three different personalities in *The Three Faces of Eve* (1957)?
a. Jane Greer **b.** Joanne Woodward **c.** Joan Leslie
d. Jeanne Crain **e.** Susan Hayward

23. *Wuthering Heights* (1939) was a classic love story starring Laurence Olivier. Can you name his co-star?
a. Bette Davis **b.** Jennifer Jones **c.** Greta Garbo
d. Merle Oberon **e.** Katharine Hepburn

24. Who starred along with Robert Stack, Dorothy Malone and Rock Hudson in *Written on the Wind* (1956)?
a. Lauren Bacall **b.** Jane Wyman **c.** Marilyn Monroe
d. Donna Reed **e.** Maureen O'Hara

25. In the classic family drama of the forties *A Tree Grows in Brooklyn* (1945), who starred as the drunken Irish father?
a. Lloyd Nolan **b.** Edmond O'Brien **c.** James Dunn
d. Victor McLaglen **e.** Jack Haley

26. Who played Barbra Streisand's husband in *The Way We Were* (1973)?
a. George Segal **b.** Ryan O'Neal **c.** Paul Newman
d. Robert Redford **e.** Steve McQueen

27. In *Love Story* (1970), Ryan O'Neal played the boy. Who played the girl?
a. Faye Dunaway **b.** Ali MacGraw **c.** Julie Christie
d. Sally Field **e.** Stefanie Powers

28. Who played Natalie Wood's boyfriend in *Love with the Proper Stranger* (1964)?
a. William Holden **b.** Rock Hudson **c.** Steve McQueen
d. Tony Curtis **e.** Stuart Whitman

29. Who starred in the film version of Somerset Maugham's popular novel *The Razor's Edge* (1947)?
a. Tyrone Power   **b.** Cornel Wilde   **c.** John Garfield
d. Errol Flynn   **e.** Spencer Tracy

30. *Middle of the Night* (1959) starred Fredric March as an elderly garment manufacturer. Who played the young woman he fell in love with?
a. Kim Novak   **b.** Eleanor Parker   **c.** Deborah Kerr   **d.** Ann Blyth   **e.** Elizabeth Taylor

31. Who starred in *Love Letters* (1945)?
a. Loretta Young   **b.** Patricia Neal   **c.** Joan Crawford
d. Myrna Loy   **e.** Jennifer Jones

32. Who starred as the advertising executive in *The Hucksters* (1947)?
a. Clark Gable   **b.** William Holden   **c.** Fred MacMurray
d. Fredric March   **e.** Van Heflin

33. Who co-starred with Ali MacGraw in *Goodbye Columbus* (1969)?
a. Steve McQueen   **b.** Elliott Gould   **c.** Ryan O'Neal
d. Richard Benjamin   **e.** Warren Beatty

34. Who played the title role in *Georgy Girl* (1966)?
a. Joan Collins   **b.** Lynn Redgrave   **c.** Sally Field
d. Vanessa Redgrave   **e.** Hayley Mills

35. Who starred in the film version of the sensational best-seller novel of the forties *Forever Amber* (1947)?
a. Linda Darnell   **b.** Rita Hayworth   **c.** Jennifer Jones
d. Susan Hayward   **e.** Gene Tierney

36. Another big novel of the forties, *Flamingo Road*, came to the screen in 1949. Who played the woman who created a sensation in a small town?

a. Betty Grable   **b.** Jane Russell   **c.** Paulette Goddard
d. Joan Crawford   **e.** Veronica Lake

37. Who starred in the film version of Arthur Miller's powerful play *Death of a Salesman* (1952)?
a. Lee J. Cobb   **b.** Henry Fonda   **c.** Fredric March   **d.** Ray Milland   **e.** Edmond O'Brien

38. Jack Lemmon starred in *Days of Wine and Roses* (1962). Who played his alcoholic wife?
a. Carolyn Jones   **b.** Lee Remick   **c.** Ann-Margret
d. Carroll Baker   **e.** Janet Leigh

39. Name the actress who starred in *The Love Machine* (1971), which was based on Jacqueline Susann's best seller.
a. Faye Dunaway   **b.** Julie Christie   **c.** Natalie Wood
d. Dyan Cannon   **e.** Raquel Welch

40. Who played the starring role of the hunter in a film based on a story by Hemingway, *The Snows of Kilimanjaro* (1952)? His leading ladies were Susan Hayward and Ava Gardner.
a. William Holden   **b.** Robert Taylor   **c.** Gregory Peck
d. Clark Gable   **e.** Stewart Granger

Name that movie!

1. This film was a remake of *Love Affair* (but that's not the title this time out). It tells the story of a girl who falls in love, on an ocean liner, with a wealthy bachelor. A number of unfortunate events prevent her from later uniting with her love. A super soaper!

THE CAST: Cary Grant, Deborah Kerr, Cathleen Nesbitt, Richard Denning

Name that movie!

2. A footloose, carefree young man is partly responsible for a young woman's blindness, and he devotes his life to trying to cure her affliction. A very well done tear-jerker. You might say it's "magnificent."

THE CAST: Irene Dunne, Robert Taylor, Ralph Morgan, Sara Haden, Charles Butterworth, Betty Furness

Name that movie!

3. This film is based on a best-selling novel by Rachel Field. It is the story of a French nobleman who falls in love with a young lady and murders his wife to be with her. Good acting, coupled with a story line that includes romance, scandal, murder and suicide, makes for high melodrama. Clue: "Heaven" is in the title.

THE CAST: Charles Boyer, Bette Davis, Barbara O'Neil, Virginia Weidler, Jeffrey Lynn, Helen Westley, Henry Daniell, Walter Hampden, Harry Davenport, George Coulouris, June Lockhart

Name that movie!

4. An aging married beauty decides to grab a new lease on life. She undergoes plastic surgery and then embarks on an uninhibited sex life and leaves her husband. An interesting slice of life from members of today's upper middle class who are attempting to burn the candle at both ends.

THE CAST: Elizabeth Taylor, Henry Fonda, Helmut Berger, Keith Baxter, Maurice Teynac

Name that movie!

5. Two ordinary middle-aged people meet at a convention in New York and fall in love. A sentimental, charming drama that touches all the right chords. Clue: It's "heart"-warming.

THE CAST: Glenn Ford, Geraldine Page, Angela Lansbury, Michael Anderson, Jr., Barbara Nichols, Patricia Barry, Charles Drake

Name that movie!

6. A man emigrates to New Zealand and sends word back home for one of two sisters to come over and be his bride. The wrong sister gets his message and pretends she is the one that he wants. Sister number two goes to New Zealand, and though he is disappointed at seeing her, she manages to get him to marry her. This film was based on a novel by Elizabeth Goudge. Clue: It's the name of a street.

THE CAST: Lana Turner, Richard Hart, Edmund Gwenn, Van Heflin, Donna Reed, Gladys Cooper

Name that movie!

7. This melodrama is based on a well-known play by Eugene O'Neill. A farmer brings home a young bride who stirs the passions of his son. The ingredients are all there, but they never come to a proper boil.

THE CAST: Sophia Loren, Burl Ives, Anthony Perkins, Frank Overton, Pernell Roberts, Anne Seymour

Name that movie!

8. A mature married woman suddenly finds herself involved in a love affair with a local acquaintance. They ultimately agree that it is best that they never see each other again. A brilliantly executed romantic drama based on a play by Noel Coward. It is a moving and memorable gem!

THE CAST: Celia Johnson, Trevor Howard, Stanley Holloway, Joyce Carey, Cyril Raymond

Name that movie!

9. A young stranger arrives in a small Kansas town one summer, and his brash sexual involvements change a number of lives. This film version of William Inge's powerful play does justice to it.

THE CAST: William Holden, Kim Novak, Rosalind Russell, Susan Strasberg, Arthur O'Connell, Cliff Robertson, Betty Field

Name that movie!

10. A middle-aged spinster marries a handsome young man who (unknown to her) is on the verge of a mental breakdown. A good "catch" isn't what it appears to be, and our born-to-suffer heroine does her thing. Female audiences went crazy for this one. Clue: It's something that happens just before the trees go bare.

THE CAST: Joan Crawford, Cliff Robertson, Lorne Greene, Vera Miles, Ruth Donnelly, Shepperd Strudwick

Name that movie!

11. A mild-mannered professor falls for a cheap (but beautiful) night club singer. She marries him and does the only thing she is capable of doing—she destroys him. Powerful and moving, this film made Dietrich an overnight sensation!

THE CAST: Emil Jannings, Marlene Dietrich, Kurt Gerron, Hans Albers, Rosa Valenti

Name that movie!

12. An unattractive Brooklyn butcher and a plain girl meet and struggle to overcome their fears of being incapable of finding true love together. A brilliant, sensitive, no-frills classic.

THE CAST: Ernest Borgnine, Betsy Blair, Esther Minciotti, Joe Mantell, Karen Steele, Jerry Paris

Name that movie!

13. A woman doggedly continues to waste her life by loving a roguish pianist who doesn't sincerely care for her. A four-handkerchief tragic melodrama. Clue: Don't open your mail box, ladies.

THE CAST: Joan Fontaine, Louis Jourdan, Mady Christians, Art Smith, Marcel Journet

Name that movie!

14. A down-on-his-luck Hollywood screen writer allows himself to be kept by a fading silent-screen movie queen who dreams of making a comeback. A big screen melodrama about Hollywood, and it's a winner!

THE CAST: Gloria Swanson, William Holden, Erich von Stroheim, Fred Clark, Nancy Olson, Jack Webb, and cameos by Cecil B. De Mille, H. B. Warner, Buster Keaton and Hedda Hopper

Name that movie!

15. A jealous woman kills her twin sister, and then steals her identity and her husband. Bette Davis displays her talents in a dual role.

THE CAST: Bette Davis, Glenn Ford, Dane Clark, Walter Brennan, Charles Ruggles, Bruce Bennett

Name that movie!

16. A great violinist, who is married, has an affair with another woman. Fine performances by a talented cast; Bergman scores big in this classic love story.

THE CAST: Leslie Howard, Ingrid Bergman, John Halliday, Edna Best, Cecil Kellaway

Name that movie!

17. A flashy society girl discovers that she is dying, and she shows her true grit in coping with her tragedy. One of Bette's famous tear-jerkers, and she delivers a dynamite performance!

THE CAST: Bette Davis, George Brent, Humphrey Bogart, Ronald Reagan, Geraldine Fitzgerald, Cora Witherspoon

Name that movie!

18. A composer leaves his rich wife for a young girl suffering from a chronic ailment. The story is based on a best seller by Margaret Kennedy. A good cast gives the story class and substance.

THE CAST: Charles Boyer, Joan Fontaine, Alexis Smith, Brenda Marshall, Charles Coburn, Dame May Whitty, Peter Lorre, Jean Muir, Joyce Reynolds

Name that movie!

19. A classic play by Edmond Rostand comes to the screen. It tells the tragic love story in the life of a seventeenth-century poet-philosopher whose physical ugliness could not hide the beauty of his soul. Find the time to see it.

THE CAST: Jose Ferrer, Mala Powers, William Prince, Morris Carnovsky, Ralph Clanton, Virginia Farmer, Edgar Barrier, Elena Verdugo

Name that movie!

20. The wife of a Russian aristocrat has an illicit romance. This film version of Leo Tolstoy's famous novel is wonderful melodrama played by a top cast. You can watch the Garbo legend in the making.

THE CAST: Greta Garbo, Fredric March, Basil Rathbone, Freddie Bartholomew, Maureen O'Sullivan, Reginald Owen, Reginald Denny

Name that movie!

True or false?

1. *The Great Gatsby* (1974) starred Paul Newman.

2. Maureen O'Hara starred in *How Green Was My Valley* (1941).

3. Lee Remick played the title role in *Harlow* (1965).

4. *Five Finger Exercise* (1962) is the story of a piano player's rise to fame.

5. In *This Sporting Life* (1963), Richard Harris played the role of a society playboy.

6. *From the Terrace* (1960), based on a novel by John O'Hara, starred Paul Newman and his wife Joanne Woodward.

7. *Lolita* (1962) told the story of a middle-aged man who falls in love with a 14-year-old girl and marries her mother just to have her near him.

8. *Robin and Marian* (1976), a film about Robin Hood in his middle age, starred Sean Connery (of James Bond fame).

9. *Husbands* (1970) starred Peter Falk.

10. Warren Beatty co-starred with Vivien Leigh in *The Roman Spring of Mrs. Stone* (1961).

11. Maureen O'Hara starred in *Ryan's Daughter* (1971) with Robert Mitchum.

12. *A Song to Remember* (1945) was the film biography of Chopin.

13. Marlon Brando starred in *A Streetcar Named Desire* (1951).

14. Laurence Olivier starred in *Summer and Smoke* (1961).

15. *Tammy and the Bachelor* (1957), a teenage romance film, starred Sandra Dee.

16. Grace Kelly, during her brief film career, appeared in two movies with Bing Crosby, *The Country Girl* (1954) and *High Society* (1956).

17. *Some Came Running* (1959), a melodrama based on a novel by James Jones, starred Frank Sinatra and Dean Martin.

18. *Valley of the Dolls* (1967) was the story of a young actress who takes to drugs when she can't cope with the pressures of show business.

19. *Women in Love* (1969) starred Glenda Jackson.

20. *X, Y and Zee* (1971) starred Elizabeth Taylor and Richard Burton.

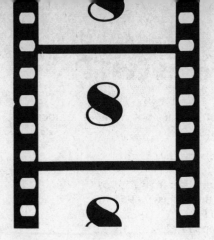

Epics

Every now and then a producer decides that a particular film project deserves "super" treatment, namely a huge production budget that is to be spent on lavish sets, a long list of stars, a cast of thousands, and much more. In Hollywood terms, he decides to make an "epic."

Epics have usually been based on a story from the Bible, a classic novel or a major historical or biographical story. These "super" flicks have usually been great spectacles, if nothing else, and many have been quite memorable films.

Now, let's find out just how memorable the epics really are— all several-hundred-million-dollars worth—as you proceed with *The Great Movie Quiz.*

Name that star!

1. He has starred in many films, but is most famous for his roles in some great epics.

FILM CREDITS: The Ten Commandments *(1956)*
Ben Hur *(1959)*
The Greatest Story Ever Told *(1965)*
The Agony and the Ecstasy *(1965)*
Julius Caesar *(1970)*
Antony and Cleopatra *(1971)*

Name that star!

2. Back in the fifties, one of Hollywood's romantic idols starred in these epics.

FILM CREDITS: Quo Vadis *(1951)*
Ivanhoe *(1952)*
Knights of the Round Table *(1953)*

Name that star!

3. This big guy always seemed at home in a big production, like a fish in water.

FILM CREDITS: One Million B.C. *(1939)*
Samson and Delilah *(1949)*
The Robe *(1953)*
Demetrius and the Gladiators *(1954)*
The Egyptian *(1954)*

Name that star!

4. A British actor (Welsh to be precise) of noteworthy ability made his mark in these productions.

FILM CREDITS: The Robe *(1953)*
Alexander the Great *(1956)*
Cleopatra *(1962)*
Becket *(1964)*
Anne of a Thousand Days *(1970)*

Name that star!

5. This athletic star seemed to love working in big productions and he always turned in a full-blooded performance.

FILM CREDITS: Ulysses *(1954)*
Lust for Life *(1956)*
The Vikings *(1958)*
Spartacus *(1960)*

Name that star!

6. This actor has a smooth but dramatic delivery of great range and he has used it to steal many scenes without so much as twitching a single face muscle.

FILM CREDITS: The Ten Commandments *(1956)*
The Brothers Karamazov *(1958)*
Solomon and Sheba *(1959)*
Taras Bulba *(1962)*
Kings of the Sun *(1963)*

Name that star!

7. A popular English leading man, he always turns in a sophisticated, gentlemanly performance.

FILM CREDITS: Julius Caesar *(1953)*
20,000 Leagues under the Sea *(1954)*
Journey to the Center of the Earth *(1959)*
Genghis Khan *(1965)*

Name that star!

8. He was a distinguished English actor who usually played stern old men of importance. He was also the narrator of *War of the Worlds*, a science fiction classic.

FILM CREDITS: Les Misérables *(1935)*
Things to Come *(1936)*
King Solomon's Mines *(1937)*
Richard III *(1955)*
Helen of Troy *(1955)*
The Ten Commandments *(1956)*

Name that star!

9. This rugged, Mexican-born star has great talent as an actor, which he demonstrates whenever he gets good material.

FILM CREDITS: Attila the Hun *(1954)*
Lust for Life *(1956)*
The Hunchback of Notre Dame *(1956)*
Lawrence of Arabia *(1962)*
Barabbas *(1962)*
The Shoes of the Fisherman *(1968)*

Name that star!

10. He was a fine British character actor whose plump face often sported a monocle. Despite his great talent, he often managed to be quite a "ham."

FILM CREDITS: The Private Life of Henry VIII *(1933)*
The Barretts of Wimpole Street *(1934)*
Les Misérables *(1935)*
Mutiny on the Bounty *(1935)*
Rembrandt *(1936)*
The Hunchback of Notre Dame *(1939)*

Name that star!

11. He is a top British star whose distinguished career on the stage and in films spans more than forty years. One of the greatest actors to ever appear on the screen, his performances are often brilliant, sensitive and flawless. He won an Academy Award for his role in *Hamlet*.

FILM CREDITS: Henry V *(1944)*
Hamlet *(1948)*
Richard III *(1956)*
Spartacus *(1960)*

Name that star!

12. He was a famous romantic star of the twenties. Though his huge talent often missed the mark, it was, nevertheless, always evident. Hollywood billed him as "the great profile."

FILM CREDITS: Moby Dick *(1930)*
Svengali *(1931)*
Romeo and Juliet *(1936)*
Marie Antoinette *(1938)*

Name that star!

13. An excellent British character actor, whose talent is second only to Olivier, he played Buckingham in *Richard III,* Sir Edward Carson in *Oscar Wilde* and Micawber in *David Copperfield.*

FILM CREDITS: Things to Come *(1936)*
Richard III *(1956)*
Exodus *(1961)*

Name that star!

14. This heavy-set versatile talent (actor-writer-director) often did fine work in front of the camera. A controversial figure at times, he is also considered a genius by many.

FILM CREDITS: Macbeth *(1948)*
Othello *(1951)*
Napoleon *(1954)*
Moby Dick *(1956)*
The Mongols *(1960)*
A Man for All Seasons *(1966)*

Name that star!

15. This stout Britisher is a versatile talent (actor-director-playwright). In *Quo Vadis* he played the role of Nero; in *Beau Brummell* he played George IV.

FILM CREDITS: Quo Vadis *(1951)*
The Egyptian *(1954)*
Spartacus *(1960)*

Name that star!

16. Today, this tall, long-faced gentleman is noted for his work in horror films. However, he has played a wide variety of roles during his career in the movies.

FILM CREDITS: Elizabeth and Essex *(1939)*
Tower of London *(1940)*
The Song of Bernadette *(1943)*
The Ten Commandments *(1956)*
The Story of Mankind *(1957)*

Name that star!

17. He was one of America's finest dramatic actors and also had a flair for comedy. He has played Mark Twain, Dr. Jekyll (and Mr. Hyde) and William Jennings Bryan in *Inherit the Wind.*

FILM CREDITS: The Sign of the Cross *(1933)*
Les Misérables *(1935)*
Anthony Adverse *(1936)*

Christopher Columbus *(1949)*
Alexander the Great *(1955)*

Name that star!

18. This gaunt, gifted character actor turned his talents to horror flicks in later years. He played Dracula in *The House of Frankenstein* (1945) and the title role in *Bluebeard* (1944). He has also scored some fine character roles in epics.

FILM CREDITS: The Sign of the Cross *(1932)*
Cleopatra *(1934)*
The Hurricane *(1937)*
The Egyptian *(1954)*
Then Ten Commandments *(1956)*

Name that star!

19. He was one of the most popular romantic swashbucklers to ever leap in front of a camera!

FILM CREDITS: The Charge of the Light Brigade *(1936)*
The Adventures of Robin Hood *(1938)*
Elizabeth and Essex *(1939)*
The Sea Hawk *(1940)*

Name that star!

20. He was a tall, suave British actor who always managed to play intelligent scoundrels and cads. He also achieved popularity in a series of films in which he played a private detective.

FILM CREDITS: Samson and Delilah *(1949)*
Ivanhoe *(1952)*
King Richard and the Crusaders *(1954)*
Solomon and Sheba *(1959)*

Name that star!

Name that star!

Multiple choice

1. Who starred in that Egyptian epic *Land of the Pharaohs* (1955)?
a. Yul Brynner   **b.** Jack Hawkins   **c.** Richard Harris
d. Stewart Granger   **e.** Cornel Wilde

2. Name the actress who starred in *Demetrius and the Gladiators* (1954).
a. Susan Hayward   **b.** Anne Baxter   **c.** Maureen O'Hara
d. Lana Turner   **e.** Paulette Goddard

3. *Cleopatra* was made in 1934 and again in 1963. Elizabeth Taylor starred in the remake, but who starred in the original version?
a. Hedy Lamarr   **b.** Jean Harlow   **c.** Claudette Colbert
d. Greta Garbo   **e.** Myrna Loy

4. Who played the role of Cleopatra in the film *Caesar and Cleopatra* (1945), which starred Claude Rains as Caesar?
a. Elizabeth Taylor   **b.** Jeanne Crain   **c.** Sophia Loren
d. Vivien Leigh   **e.** Gene Tierney

5. Who played the role of Solomon in *Solomon and Sheba* (1959)?
a. Yul Brynner   **b.** Gregory Peck   **c.** Charlton Heston
d. Cedric Hardwicke   **e.** George Sanders

6. Name the actress who starred in *The Robe* (1953).
a. Jean Simmons   **b.** Joan Leslie   **c.** Deborah
Kerr   **d.** Teresa Wright   **e.** Jane Wyman

7. Who starred in Cecil B. De Mille's epic *The Sign of the Cross* (1932)?
a. Ronald Colman   **b.** Spencer Tracy   **c.** Raymond Massey
d. Fredric March   **e.** Laurence Olivier

8. Name the actor who starred as the evil magician in *The Thief of Bagdad* (1940).
a. Conrad Veidt   **b.** George Sanders   **c.** Boris Karloff
d. John Carradine   **e.** Walter Slezak

9. Who was the star of the epic romance *Jane Eyre* (1944)?
a. Joan Fontaine   **b.** Olivia De Havilland   **c.** Bette Davis
d. Katharine Hepburn   **e.** Barbara Stanwyck

10. Who played the role of Christ in *The Greatest Story Ever Told* (1965)?
a. Jeffrey Hunter   **b.** John Carradine   **c.** Farley Granger
d. Max Von Sydow   **e.** John Phillip Law

11. Who played Caesar in *Julius Caesar* (1953)?
a. Louis Calhern   **b.** Claude Rains   **c.** Rex
Harrison   **d.** Fredric March   **e.** Cedric Hardwicke

12. Who played the romantic lead and boyfriend of Fay Wray in *King Kong* (1933)?
a. Warner Baxter   **b.** Bruce Cabot   **c.** Jon Hall   **d.** James
Gleason   **e.** William Gargan

13. Which one of these actresses starred in *The Towering Inferno* (1974)?
a. Ava Gardner   **b.** Karen Black   **c.** Jacqueline Bisset
d. Jean Seberg   **e.** Faye Dunaway

14. Who co-starred with Peter O'Toole in *Lawrence of Arabia* (1962)?
a. Charlton Heston   **b.** Fernando Lamas   **c.** Omar Sharif
d. Laurence Olivier   **e.** David Niven

15. In the classic *Mutiny on the Bounty* (1935), who starred as the captain of the *Bounty?*
a. Edward G. Robinson   **b.** Charles Bickford   **c.** Donald
Crisp   **d.** Charles Laughton   **e.** Lionel Barrymore

16. Name the actress who starred with Henry Wilcoxon in the historical epic *The Crusades* (1935).
a. Loretta Young   **b.** Claudette Colbert   **c.** Joan Fontaine
d. Irene Dunne   **e.** Bette Davis

17. *Salome* (1953) starred a glamorous actress who had a reputation as a dancer. What was her name?
a. Ginger Rogers   **b.** Cyd Charisse   **c.** Ann Miller   **d.** Rita Hayworth   **e.** Betty Grable

18. In *The Knights of the Round Table* (1953), who played Lady Guinevere?
a. Deborah Kerr   **b.** Ava Gardner   **c.** Maureen O'Hara
d. Lana Turner   **e.** Merle Oberon

19. In the classic film version of that classic novel *David Copperfield* (1935), who played the role of Mr. Micawber?
a. Charles Laughton   **b.** W. C. Fields   **c.** Charles Coburn
d. Edmund Gwenn   **e.** Walter Huston

20. In the first of the James Bond flicks, *Doctor No* (1962), who played the title role?
a. Joseph Wiseman   **b.** Dean Jagger   **c.** Christopher Lee
d. Raf Vallone   **e.** Adolfo Celi

21. The female lead in *Quo Vadis* (1951) was _____?
a. Elizabeth Taylor   **b.** Barbara Stanwyck   **c.** Deborah Kerr
d. Joan Fontaine   **e.** Anne Baxter

22. Who starred in the 1939 version of *The Hunchback of Notre Dame?*
a. John Carradine   **b.** Charles Laughton   **c.** John Barrymore   **d.** Anothony Quinn   **e.** Lon Chaney

23. The great Chicago fire was the highlight of *In Old Chicago* (1938). Who starred with Tyrone Power in this early epic?
a. Linda Darnell   **b.** Betty Grable   **c.** Alice Faye   **d.** Joan Blondell   **e.** Marlene Dietrich

24. *San Francisco* (1936), the story of the Frisco quake of 1906, starred Clark Gable. Who co-starred?
a. Melvyn Douglas   **b.** Spencer Tracy   **c.** Cesar Romero
d. Lloyd Nolan   **e.** Pat O'Brien

25. Who starred in *King of Kings* (1961)?
a. Anthony Perkins   **b.** Van Heflin   **c.** Jeffrey Hunter
d. Paul Newman   **e.** Laurence Harvey

26. Name the star of the 1950 remake of *King Solomon's Mines.*
a. Stewart Granger   **b.** Gary Cooper   **c.** Charlton Heston
d. Jeff Chandler   **e.** Robert Taylor

27. The remake of *Kismet* (1944)—not the 1955 musical version—starred Ronald Colman. Who was his co-star?
a. Joan Crawford   **b.** Rita Hayworth   **c.** Greta Garbo
d. Marlene Dietrich   **e.** Myrna Loy

28. The epic film version of Dickens' novel *Great Expectations* (1946) starred _____?
a. Spencer Tracy   **b.** John Mills   **c.** Robert Young
d. Charles Laughton   **e.** Laurence Olivier

29. Who starred in *The Fall of the Roman Empire* (1964)?
a. Rex Harrison   **b.** Richard Burton   **c.** Alec Guinness
d. Charlton Heston   **e.** James Mason

30. In the film version of the classic Russian novel *The Brothers Karamazov* (1958), who starred?
a. Anthony Quinn   **b.** Yul Brynner   **c.** Glenn Ford
d. Fredric March   **e.** Douglas Fairbanks, Jr.

31. Who starred in *The Red Badge of Courage* (1951), an American epic about the Civil War?
a. Dana Andrews   **b.** Gary Cooper   **c.** Audie Murphy
d. Richard Widmark   **e.** Gregory Peck

32. Who co-starred with Henry Fonda in *War and Peace* (1956)?
a. Lana Turner   **b.** Bette Davis   **c.** Loretta Young
d. Audrey Hepburn   **e.** Merle Oberon

33. Name the actress who starred in *Hawaii* (1966).
a. Shirley Jones   **b.** Leslie Caron   **c.** Shirley MacLaine
d. Deborah Kerr   **e.** Julie Andrews

34. *Doctor Zhivago* (1965), a story set in Russia during the first World War, starred Omar Sharif and _____?
a. Elizabeth Taylor   **b.** Ava Gardner   **c.** Julie Christie
d. Maureen O'Hara   **e.** Rita Hayworth

35. Ayn Rand's epic novel *The Fountainhead* came to the big screen in 1949. Who starred?
a. Clark Gable   **b.** Gary Cooper   **c.** Robert Taylor
d. Ronald Colman   **e.** Tyrone Power

36. A modernized version of the gothic novel *The Four Horsemen of the Apocalypse* was released in 1961. Name the actor who starred in it.
a. Glenn Ford   **b.** David Niven   **c.** Gregory Peck   **d.** Robert Young   **e.** William Holden

37. *Giant* (1956) told the story of two generations of a Texas cattle rancher's family. Who co-starred with Elizabeth Taylor?
a. Rock Hudson   **b.** Kirk Douglas   **c.** John Wayne
d. Henry Fonda   **e.** Burt Lancaster

38. Who starred in the original film version of Dickens' classic *A Tale of Two Cities* (1935)?
a. Fredric March   **b.** Spencer Tracy   **c.** Paul Muni
d. Ronald Colman   **e.** Paul Lukas

39. The life of Sigmund Freud came to the screen in *Freud* (1963). Who played the title role?
a. Edward G. Robinson **b.** James Mason **c.** Montgomery Clift **d.** Peter O'Toole **e.** Laurence Harvey

40. *Les Misérables* (1935), the film version of Victor Hugo's famous novel, starred Charles Laughton and _____?
a. Spencer Tracy **b.** Fredric March **c.** Walter Huston
d. John Barrymore **e.** Basil Rathbone

Name that movie!

1. Michelangelo paints the ceiling of the Sistine Chapel for Pope Julius II. Good, but it should have been great.

THE CAST: Charlton Heston, Rex Harrison, Diane Cilento, Harry Andrews, Alberto Lupo, Adolfo Celi

Name that movie!

2. This epic is best remembered for its chariot-race sequence. Excellent—one of the biggies that is worth the price of admission any time.

THE CAST: Charlton Heston, Haya Harareet, Jack Hawkins, Stephen Boyd, Hugh Griffith, Martha Scott, Sam Jaffe, Finlay Currie, Cathy O'Donnell

Name that movie!

3. The story of one of Jesus' garments that is passed on to others after his crucifixion and affects the lives of his followers and opponents. A fine production that holds your interest from start to finish.

THE CAST: Richard Burton, Jean Simmons, Michael Rennie, Victor Mature, Dean Jagger, Richard Boone, Jeff Morrow

Name that movie!

4. Fire traps a group of people in the world's tallest building. A four-alarm spectacular thriller.

THE CAST: Paul Newman, Steve McQueen, William Holden, Faye Dunaway, Fred Astaire, Susan Blakely, Richard Chamberlain, Robert Vaughn, Jennifer Jones, O. J. Simpson, Robert Wagner

Name that movie!

5. The story of the Old Testament from Adam up to Isaac, with Noah's Ark the highlight. Great scenery, but otherwise uninspired.

THE CAST: Michael Parks, Ulla Bergryd, Richard Harris, John Huston, Stephen Boyd, George C. Scott, Ava Gardner, Peter O'Toole

Name that movie!

6. The story of the boldest, roughest, toughest sailors of ancient times. A good action epic.

THE CAST: Kirk Douglas, Tony Curtis, Ernest Borgnine, Janet Leigh

Name that movie!

7. The epic tale of the best man with a paint brush in the seventeenth century. Absolutely great, and it's a fine film about a master painter.

THE CAST: Charles Laughton, Edward Chapman, Gertrude Lawrence, Elsa Lanchester, Roger Livesey, Walter Hudd

Name that movie!

8. "Beware of Greeks bearing gifts" was the moral of this historical spectacular. Homer's version was far superior.

THE CAST: Rosanna Podesta, Jacques Sernas, Cedric Hardwicke, Stanley Baker, Brigitte Bardot, Robert Wise, Harry Andrews

Name that movie!

9. According to the Bible, this epic is law. A classic!

THE CAST: Charlton Heston, Yul Brynner, Edward G. Robinson, Anne Baxter, Nina Foch, Yvonne De Carlo, John Derek, H. B. Warner, Judith Anderson, John Carradine, Douglas Dumbrille, Cedric Hardwicke, Martha Scott, Vincent Price

Name that movie!

10. The life of the famous painter Vincent Van Gogh is brought to the big screen. Interesting and worth watching.

THE CAST: Kirk Douglas, Anthony Quinn, James Donald, Pamela Brown, Everett Sloane

Name that movie!

11. The story of the Macedonian warrior who conquered all the known world in his day. He had a great deal more success than this epic did.

THE CAST: Richard Burton, Fredric March, Danielle Darrieux, Claire Bloom, Barry Jones, Harry Andrews, Peter Cushing, Stanley Baker

Name that movie!

12. Based on a popular novel, this film tells the story of a boy in ancient Egypt who grows up to become the physician to the Pharaoh. An epic, but not one of the greats.

THE CAST: Edmund Purdom, Victor Mature, Peter Ustinov, Bella Darvi, Gene Tierney, Michael Wilding, Jean Simmons

Name that movie!

13. The story of a legendary hero who drove the Moors from Spain during the eleventh century. A huge, gloomy epic with some great action scenes.

THE CAST: Charlton Heston, Sophia Loren, Raf Vallone, Genevieve Page, Herbert Lom, Hurd Hatfield

Name that movie!

14. A brooding sea captain goes fishing with a vengeance. This is a great adventure yarn based on a classic novel, though the story is more interesting and exciting than the cast.

THE CAST: Gregory Peck, Richard Basehart, Leo Genn, Orson Welles, James Robertson Justice, Harry Andrews

Name that movie!

15. An H. G. Wells fictionalized history of the world from 1940 into the future. First, world war and the destruction of civilization. Later, a rebirth of society with scientific marvels, including a glass-enclosed city and the firing of the first rocket-ship to the Moon. (Amazing, considering that this epic was released in 1936!) In many ways, this is the most interesting and brilliant film epic ever produced.

THE CAST: Raymond Massey, Edward Chapman, Ralph Richardson, Margaretta Scott, Cedric Hardwicke, Maurice Bradell, Sophia Stewart

Name that movie!

16. A look at the life of primitive man, clubs, caves and dinosaurs. Well done, and its unusual subject matter makes it all pure entertainment.

THE CAST: Victor Mature, Carole Landis, Lon Chaney, Jr., John Hubbard

Name that movie!

17. A terrible monsoon strikes in India, and a group of seemingly worthless characters rise to the occasion during the flood disaster. A fine cast and a thrilling disaster epic.

THE CAST: Myrna Loy, George Brent, Tyrone Power, Brenda Joyce, Maria Ouspenskaya, Joseph Schildkaut, H. B. Warner, Nigel Bruce, Mary Nash, Jane Darwell, Henry Travers, Marjorie Rambeau

Name that movie!

18. Mount Vesuvius blows its top! The mountain deserves top billing in this one.

THE CAST: Preston Foster, Basil Rathbone, Alan Hale, Dorothy Wilson, Gloria Shea

Name that movie!

19. Bernard Shaw's play about Julius Caesar's years in Egypt is brought to the screen in a spectacular production. A fine cast and a great spectacle.

THE CAST: Claude Rains, Vivien Leigh, Cecil Parker, Stewart Granger, Flora Robson, Francis L. Sullivan

Name that movie!

20. A genie, a flying carpet, some magic and some magnificent sets make this Arabian fairy tale come to life. An enjoyable and timeless classic!

THE CAST: Conrad Veidt, Sabu, John Justin, June Duprez, Mary Morris, Miles Malleson, Rex Ingram

Name that movie!

True or false?

1. Cecil B. De Mille produced and directed *The Ten Commandments* (1956).

2. Epics based on the New Testament include: *The Robe, The Sign of the Cross, The Big Fisherman* and *Ben Hur.*

3. Epics based on the Old Testament include: *A Story of David, Samson and Delilah, The Ten Commandments* and *The Story of Ruth.*

4. Claude Rains played the role of Caesar in *Caesar and Cleopatra* (1945).

5. Richard Harris played the role of Cain in *The Bible* (1966).

6. Elizabeth Taylor, Richard Burton and Rex Harrison all starred together in *Cleopatra* (1963).

7. *The Crusades* (1935) told the story of the holy wars of King Richard the Lionheart.

8. *Genghis Khan* (1964) starred Orson Welles.

9. *Great Expectations* (1946) was a British epic and not a Hollywood production.

10. Laurence Olivier starred in *Hamlet* (1948) and Orson Welles directed this classic.

11. *The Hunchback of Notre Dame* (1938) told the story of a deformed church-bell ringer.

12. *Joan of Arc* (1948) starred Ingrid Bergman.

13. *Julius Caesar* (1953) starred Cedric Hardwicke.

14. *Land of the Pharaohs* (1955) starred Jack Hawkins.

15. *Lawrence of Arabia* (1962) starred Richard Burton.

16. *Little Caesar* (1930) was the story of Julius Caesar's childhood.

17. *Lloyds of London* (1936) told the story of the founding of a world-famous jeweler.

18. The actress who starred in *Richard III* (1956) was Claire Bloom.

19. *The Sign of the Pagan* (1954) was the story of Attila the Hun.

20. *The Silver Chalice* (1955) starred Victor Mature.

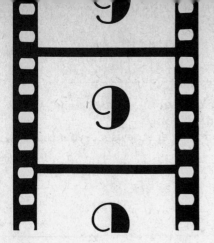

Science Fiction

Today, the science fiction film has really come into its own as a major film category. Why? For one thing, the biggest-grossing film of all time is *Star Wars!* And *Star Wars* wasn't just an accident. Ever since *2001: A Space Odyssey,* a growing number of big-budget science fiction films have done very well at the box office, e.g., *Planet of the Apes* and its sequels, *The Andromeda Strain* and *Close Encounters of the Third Kind.*

Perhaps the advent of space exploration and the growth in popularity of science fiction literature have been the major factors in building a loyal audience. The incredible success of the James Bond film series (certainly a form of science fiction film) tells movie makers that the general public wants science fiction adventure in a big way.

Now, let's put greatest computer ever devised—your brain—to work on our quiz!

Name that star!

NOTE: Since most actors and actresses have not appeared in many science fiction films during their careers, we are going to help you identify them by listing some of their credits in other film genres. The science fiction credits will be shown in bold-face type.

1. This attractive blonde was a popular actress in the fifties. She usually appeared in low-budget films.

FILM CREDITS: **The Rocket Man** *(1954)*
It Conquered the World *(1956)*
Not of This Earth *(1957)*
The Alligator People *(1959)*
Twice-Told Tales *(1963)*

Name that star!

2. This American leading man usually plays scientists and intelligent heroic types.

FILM CREDITS: The Robe *(1953)*
This Island Earth *(1955)*
The Creature Walks Among Us *(1956)*
The Giant Claw *(1957)*
Kronos *(1957)*
The Story of Ruth *(1960)*

Name that star!

3. He has appeared in varied roles in films, but he has managed to make a career for himself in science fiction flicks. He usually plays scientists and scholarly adventuresome types.

FILM CREDITS: King Solomon's Mines *(1950)*
The Magnetic Monster *(1953)*
It Came from Outer Space *(1953)*
Riders to the Stars *(1954)*
The Creature from the Black Lagoon *(1954)*
The Helen Morgan Story *(1957)*
The Power *(1968)*
The Valley of Gwangi *(1969)*

Name that star!

4. This attractive, dark-haired leading lady appeared in a variety of films in the fifties and sixties. Clue: Her last name rhymes with "brush."

FILM CREDITS: **When Worlds Collide** *(1951)*
It Came from Outer Space *(1953)*
Come Blow Your Horn *(1963)*
Robin and the Seven Hoods *(1964)*
Hombre *(1967)*

Name that star!

5. This actor has had a long and distinguished career in films. He always plays a quiet, dignified man of character.

FILM CREDITS: Dark Command *(1940)*
Madame Curie *(1943)*
Executive Suite *(1954)*
Forbidden Planet *(1956)*
Voyage to the Bottom of the Sea *(1961)*
Advise and Consent *(1962)*

Name that star!

6. He was a popular leading man in the thirties, forties and fifties. One of Hollywood's most durable stars, he now plays elderly fathers and uncles.

FILM CREDITS: Ministry of Fear *(1944)*
Alias Nick Beal *(1949)*
Dial M for Murder *(1954)*
Panic in the Year Zero *(1962)*
The Man with X-Ray Eyes *(1963)*
Love Story *(1970)*
Frogs *(1972)*

Name that star!

7. This leading man is one of filmdom's top stars today. He has played a wide range of roles and is most remembered for his work in epic films.

FILM CREDITS: The War Lord *(1965)*
Khartoum *(1966)*
Will Penny *(1968)*
Beneath the Planet of the Apes *(1969)*
The Omega Man *(1971)*
Soylent Green *(1973)*

Name that star!

8. This burly, blond leading man is an Australian who came to Hollywood. He usually plays adventurers and nice tough guys.

FILM CREDITS: **The Time Machine** *(1960)*
The Birds *(1963)*
The Liquidator *(1965)*
Darker Than Amber *(1970)*
Trader Horn *(1973)*

Name that star!

9. This attractive English actress became closely associated with horror films in the fifties and sixties.

FILM CREDITS: Cat Girl *(1957)*
Village of the Damned *(1961)*
The Gorgon *(1964)*
Dracula, Prince of Darkness *(1965)*
Quatermass and the Pit *(1967)*

Name that star!

10. This actor made a career of starring in low-budget science fiction films. However, he was also a supporting player in two John Wayne westerns: *The Undefeated* and *Big Jake*.

FILM CREDITS: The Brain from Planet Arous *(1948)*
Revenge of the Creature *(1955)*
Tarantula *(1955)*
The Mole People *(1956)*
Journey of the Seventh Planet *(1961)*
Zantar: The Thing from Venus *(1967)*

Name that star!

11. This tall leading man starred in the Perry Mason TV series as private eye Paul Drake.

FILM CREDITS: Track of the Cat *(1954)*
Conquest of Space *(1955)*
The Bad Seed *(1956)*
The Deadly Mantis *(1957)*
Twenty Million Miles to Earth *(1957)*

Name that star!

12. He is a tall, lean English leading man with high cheekbones and a poised, intelligent manner.

FILM CREDITS: Les Misérables *(1952)*
The Day the Earth Stood Still *(1952)*
Omar Khayyam *(1957)*

The Lost World *(1960)*
The Power *(1967)*
The Devil's Brigade *(1968)*

Name that star!

13. A tall, blond actor who plays both good and bad guys, scientists and weirdos.

FILM CREDITS: Rachel, Rachel *(1967)*
The Andromeda Strain *(1970)*
Moon Zero Two *(1970)*
Wild Rovers *(1971)*
The Groundstar Conspiracy *(1972)*

Name that star!

14. This handsome, long-jawed American actor is currently appearing in a TV soap opera. He has had varied roles in films.

FILM CREDITS: Twelve O'Clock High *(1950)*
All About Eve *(1950)*
The Day the Earth Stood Still *(1951)*
Earth Versus the Flying Saucers *(1956)*
World Without End *(1956)*

Name that star!

15. This attractive British leading lady is quite popular today. She has appeared in a number of American films.

FILM CREDITS: Billy Liar *(1963)*
Darling *(1965)*
Doctor Zhivago *(1966)*
Fahrenheit 451 *(1966)*
Demon Seed *(1977)*

Name that star!

16. He is a tall, dignified actor with a gentle voice. He has made a notable career for himself by starring in numerous horror films.

FILM CREDITS: **The Invisible Man Returns** *(1939)*
House of Wax *(1953)*
The Mad Magician *(1954)*
The Fly *(1958)*
The Fall of the House of Usher *(1961)*
Master of the World *(1961)*

Name that star!

17. This gaunt English actor is known for his long career in horror films. He usually plays a scientist or doctor who gets involved with things better left alone.

FILM CREDITS: **The Abominable Snowman** *(1957)*
Dracula *(1959)*
The Mummy *(1959)*
She *(1965)*
Dr. Who and the Daleks *(1965)*
The Skull *(1965)*
Tales from the Crypt *(1971)*
Star Wars *(1978)*

Name that star!

18. He is a suave American actor with sharp features and a pencil mustache. He has played supporting roles in a number of films.

FILM CREDITS: Spellbound *(1945)*
Blood on the Sun *(1945)*
Rocketship X-M *(1950)*
Ten North Frederick *(1957)*
Kronos *(1957)*

Name that star!

19. This short, talented young American actor burst onto the big screen in the seventies when he appeared in several box-office winners.

FILM CREDITS: American Graffiti *(1973)*
Jaws *(1975)*
Close Encounters of the Third Kind *(1977)*

Name that star!

20. This debonair American actor played Bat Masterson in a TV series and starred in a major science fiction classic.

FILM CREDITS: **The War of the Worlds** *(1953)*
Red Garters *(1954)*
Naked Alibi *(1954)*
The 27th Day *(1957)*
China Gate *(1957)*
Thunder Road *(1958)*

Name that star!

Name that star!

Multiple choice

1. Who starred in *Village of the Damned* (1960)?
a. Herbert Marshall   **b.** Marshall Thompson   **c.** Vic Morrow
d. George Sanders   **e.** Warner Anderson

2. Which one of these actors starred in *Red Planet Mars* (1952)?
a. Arthur Franz   **b.** Gerald Mohr   **c.** Peter Graves   **d.** Richard Carlson   **e.** Jeffrey Hunter

3. Which of these actors was featured in *Riders to the Stars* (1954)?
a. Tom Drake   **b.** William Lundigan   **c.** Craig Stevens
d. William Hopper   **e.** Rod Taylor

4. In *The Creeping Unknown* (1955)—the American title of the British film *The Quatermass Experiment*—who played the role of Quatermass?
a. Steve McQueen   **b.** Brian Donlevy   **c.** MacDonald Carey
d. Dana Andrews   **e.** Gene Evans

5. Who co-starred with George Sanders and Debra Paget in *From Earth to the Moon* (1958)?
a. Joseph Cotten   **b.** Kirk Douglas   **c.** Charles Bronson
d. Edmond O'Brien   **e.** James Whitmore

6. *Destination Moon* (1950) starred Warner Anderson and _____?
a. Richard Carlson   **b.** Hugh Marlowe   **c.** John Emery
d. Sterling Hayden   **e.** John Archer

7. Name the actress who played the role of Dr. Morbius's daughter in *Forbidden Planet* (1956).
a. Barbara Rush   **b.** Julie Adams   **c.** Anne Francis   **d.** Martha Hyer   **e.** Mara Corday

8. Who starred in *First Man into Space* (1958)?
a. Leslie Nielsen   **b.** Warren Stevens   **c.** Tom Tryon
d. Marshall Thompson   **e.** Richard Denning

9. Who was the famous English actor who served as the unseen narrator of *War of the Worlds* (1952)?
a. Ralph Richardson   **b.** Alec Guinness   **c.** John Gielgud
d. James Mason   **e.** Cedric Hardwicke

10. Who starred as the submarine commander in *On the Beach* (1959)?
a. Richard Widmark   **b.** William Holden   **c.** Burt Lancaster
d. Glenn Ford   **e.** Gregory Peck

11. The film version of Jules Verne's classic science fiction novel *Journey to the Center of the Earth* (1959), starred _____?
a. Walter Pidgeon   **b.** Kirk Douglas   **c.** James Mason
d. Vincent Price   **e.** David Niven

12. Name the star of *The Man Who Fell to Earth* (1976).
a. Keir Dullea   **b.** David Bowie   **c.** George
Peppard   **d.** Dennis Hopper   **e.** Richard Benjamin

13. In *Futureworld* (1976), a sequel to *Westworld* (1973), who starred?
a. Yul Brynner   **b.** George Segal   **c.** Peter
Fonda   **d.** Warren Beatty   **e.** Chris Connelly

14. Who starred in the film version of Ray Bradbury's, *The Illustrated Man* (1968)?
a. Marlon Brando   **b.** Burt Lancaster   **c.** Rod Steiger
d. Kirk Douglas   **e.** George C. Scott

15. *The Damned* (1963) was a film about some children who were deliberately isolated and exposed to atomic radiation. Who starred?

---

a. MacDonald Carey **b.** Ben Johnson **c.** Edmond O'Brien
d. Glenn Ford **e.** William Holden

16. Who played the title role (and two other roles) in *Dr. Strangelove: Or, How I Learned to Stop Worrying and Love the Bomb* (1963)?
a. Peter Sellers **b.** Alec Guinness **c.** David
Niven **d.** George C. Scott **e.** Anthony Newley

17. George Lucas, of *Star Wars* fame, produced a science fiction film called *THX 1138* (1971). Who starred in it?
a. Robert Duvall **b.** Doug McClure **c.** James Olson
d. Earl Holliman **e.** Leslie Nielsen

18. Who starred in *Zardoz* (1974)?
a. Michael Sarrazin **b.** Sean Connery **c.** James Caan
d. Michael Caine **e.** James Coburn

19. *The Food of the Gods* (1976) was based on a story by H. G. Wells. Who starred in this film?
a. James Whitmore **b.** Robert Foxworth **c.** Martin Sheen
d. Marjoe Gortner **e.** Donald Pleasance

20. Who was the champion player in the sport of the future called *Rollerball* (1975)?
a. David Janssen **b.** James Caan **c.** Robert Redford
d. Burt Reynolds **e.** Robert Culp

21. Who starred as the spaceflight mission controller in *Marooned* (1969)?
a. James Stewart **b.** Brian Keith **c.** Gregory
Peck **d.** George Kennedy **e.** Robert Preston

22. Name the actress who starred in *Fantastic Voyage* (1966).
a. Raquel Welch **b.** Julie Christie **c.** Ann-Margret
d. Faye Dunaway **e.** Lee Remick

23. Who played the starring role of a "fireman" in *Fahrenheit 451* (1966)?
a. Gene Barry **b.** Oskar Werner **c.** Cliff Robertson
d. Don Murray **e.** Richard Todd

24. Who starred as Professor Cavor in *First Men in the Moon* (1960)?
a. Lionel Jeffries **b.** Vincent Price **c.** Walter Pidgeon
d. Herbert Lom **e.** Peter Lorre

25. In *20,000 Leagues under the Sea* (1954), who played the role of Captain Nemo?
a. Herbert Lom **b.** James Mason **c.** Orson Welles
d. Telly Savalas **e.** Jose Ferrer

26. Aliens from a doomed planet plan to invade Earth in *The Man from Planet X* (1951). Who plays the news reporter who thwarts them?
a. Hugh O'Brian **b.** Robert Clarke **c.** Edward Franz
d. James Arness **e.** William Hopper

27. Name the actor who played the title role in *Dr. Cyclops* (1940).
a. Yul Brynner **b.** Donald Pleasance **c.** Peter Lorre
d. Albert Dekker **e.** Dean Jagger

28. Who starred in *Atlantis, the Lost Continent* (1961)?
a. Fernando Lamas **b.** Anthony Hall **c.** Jon
Hall **d.** Michael Rennie **e.** Richard Greene

29. In *Crack in the World* (1965), who starred as the scientist whose missile nearly destroys the world?
a. Vincent Price **b.** Paul Lukas **c.** Dana Andrews **d.** John
Huston **e.** Paul Burke

30. Name the star of *The Day of the Triffids* (1962).
a. Rod Taylor **b.** Gordon MacRae **c.** Howard
Keel **d.** Barry Sullivan **e.** David Janssen

31. Who starred in the British-made science fiction thriller titled *The Day the Earth Caught Fire* (1961)?
a. Edward Judd   **b.** Trevor Howard   **c.** John Mills   **d.** Peter O'Toole   **e.** Michael Redgrave

32. *The Stepford Wives* (1974) tells the chilling tale of how all the wives in a small town are being replaced by perfect robot duplicates—with the knowledge and consent of all the husbands. Who starred?
a. Katharine Ross   **b.** Natalie Wood   **c.** Barbara Parkins
d. Diane Baker   **e.** Martha Hyer

33. *Chosen Survivors* (1974) is the story of ten people who have been selected to test human reaction to a nuclear holocaust. Who starred along with Alex Cord, Richard Jaeckel and Diana Muldaur?
a. James Franciscus   **b.** Roddy McDowall   **c.** Rod Taylor
d. Jackie Cooper   **e.** Glenn Corbett

34. *Sleeper* (1973) was a science fiction comedy. Who starred?
a. Art Carney   **b.** Jerry Lewis   **c.** Woody Allen   **d.** Mel Brooks   **e.** Gene Wilder

35. Who played the role of Flash Gordon in *Flash Gordon Conquers the Universe* (1940)?
a. Bruce Cabot   **b.** Buster Crabbe   **c.** Anthony Dexter
d. William Gargan   **e.** John Howard

36. Who starred in the film version of George Orwell's disturbing look into the future, *1984* (1956)?
a. Charlton Heston   **b.** Spencer Tracy   **c.** Trevor Howard
d. Robert Ryan   **e.** Edmond O'Brien

37. Name the actor who played *The Invisible Man* (1933).
a. Boris Karloff   **b.** Peter Lorre   **c.** William Powell   **d.** Claude Rains   **e.** Basil Rathbone

38. Which one of these actors played the title role in *The Incredible Shrinking Man* (1957)?
a. Charles Drake   **b.** Grant Williams   **c.** Gene Nelson
d. Clu Gulager   **e.** Howard Duff

39. Channeling human aggressions into a murderous game called "The Hunt" is the futuristic story told in *The Tenth Victim* (1965). Who co-starred with Marcello Mastroianni in this film?
a. Sophia Loren   **b.** Gina Lollobrigida   **c.** Ursula Andress
d. Virna Lisi   **e.** Jane Fonda

40. In *Planet of the Apes* (1968), who played the role of the ape named Cornelius that befriended Charlton Heston?
a. Sal Mineo   **b.** Roddy McDowall   **c.** Strother Martin
d. James Whitmore   **e.** Gary Lockwood

Name that movie!

1. Seeds from outer space land in a small town. They begin growing into duplicates of the townspeople and replacing them after taking over their minds. Our hero learns what's happening, but he can't get anyone to believe that there is "a seed of truth" to his story. A low-budget classic!

THE CAST: Kevin McCarthy, Dana Wynter, Larry Gates, King Donovan, Carolyn Jones, Virginia Christine

Name that movie!

2. A huge alien spaceship lands in Mexico. It then proceeds to travel across the country toward the United States, stopping at every major power facility and draining away all of the stored power. The mission of this alien device is to drain and store all Earth's atomic and electrical power and take it back to its energy-starved home planet. Don't examine the concept too closely and it's fun to watch.

THE CAST: Jeff Morrow, Barbara Lawrence, John Emery, Morris Ankrum

Name that movie!

3. A flying saucer crashes in the Arctic, and a strange alien is found frozen in the ice near the crash site. Once unthawed, this alien turns out to be a humanoid-vegetable which proceeds to kill the members of the search party who have found him and then feeds on their blood. An absolutely chilling science fiction classic!

THE CAST: Robert Cornthwaite, Kenneth Tobey, Margaret Sheridan, Bill Self, Dewey Martin, James Arness

Name that movie!

4. An alien virus is brought back to Earth by a space probe that crashes near a small desert town. All of the town's inhabitants are killed almost instantly with only two exceptions: a drunk and a baby. Scientists isolate the survivors and race against time to try to learn how to combat this alien killer virus. An exciting, well-done film—not a classic, but close.

THE CAST: Arthur Hill, David Wayne, James Olson, Kate Reid, Paula Kelly

Name that movie!

5. A huge flying saucer lands on the lawn of the White House. A humanoid alien and a large metallic robot appear to make contact with Earth. Unfamiliar with Washington politics, the alien is soon at odds with the frightened and suspicious authorities. A military show of force against the alien is fruitless, and to further demonstrate his superiority, he causes all of Earth's nonessential machines, motors and vehicles to come to a halt. (An environmentalist's dream!) Good premise. It should have been great—but wasn't.

THE CAST: Michael Rennie, Patricia Neal, Hugh Marlowe, Sam Jaffe, Billy Gray

Name that movie!

6. A young boy sees a flying saucer land and later realizes that his family and the townspeople have become "different"— they are all under the influence of an alien force. He finally convinces the authorities of what is going on and the military is called in to destroy the underground lair set up by these aliens. Then comes the double-twist ending: it all turns out to be just a boy's dream—which is now about to really happen! Pretty good low-budget stuff.

THE CAST: Jimmy Hunt, Leif Erickson, Helena Carter

Name that movie!

7. An alien visitor turns up wearing heavy dark glasses as his only disguise. He busily goes about collecting human plasma for the folks back home, where radioactivity in their blood is wiping them out. Very anemic.

THE CAST: Paul Birch, Beverly Garland, Morgan Jones, William Roerick

Name that movie!

8. Excavation workers in the London subway system unearth a spaceship and the remains of alien creatures buried there since prehistoric times. Scientists discover that this spaceship is still in working order. When activated, the ship conjures up a huge transparent vision of its makers that draws upon the mental energy of the city's inhabitants in an attempt to conquer mankind. Excellent story ranks this one among the best.

THE CAST: Andrew Keir, James Donald, Barbara Shelley, Julian Glover, Maurice Good

Name that movie!

9. All the women in an English country village are impregnated by some alien force and give birth to a group of quiet, blond children with incredible mental powers. A good science fiction film.

THE CAST: George Sanders, Barbara Shelley, Michael Gwynne, Martin Stephens, Laurence Naismith

Name that movie!

10. This film opens in the prehistoric time of the apes. It then leaps into the future, taking us first to an incredible space station, then on a trip to the moon, and finally on a long voyage out to the planet Jupiter. In each sequence, there is a discovery of an enigmatic monolith that has been left by some unknown advanced race for evolving mankind to discover. One of our science fiction classics!

THE CAST: Keir Dullea, Gary Lockwood, William Sylvester, Anne Gillis, Margaret Tyzack, Daniel Richter, Douglas Rain

Name that movie!

11. Aliens who are losing an interplanetary war set up a base on Earth. They lure top scientists to work with them on an energy breakthrough that will aid them in their war. The plan fails, and the alien leader, along with two of the scientists, returns home—just in time to witness the final destruction of his planet. With a little more attention to the story and special effects, it could have been a sci-fi classic.

THE CAST: Jeff Morrow, Faith Domergue, Rex Reason, Lance Fuller, Russell Johnson

Name that movie!

12. A space party from Earth visits a distant planet in another galaxy to determine the fate of an Earth colony that was started there years ago. All the colonists have been killed mysteriously, except for one of the scientists and his daughter. The surviving scientist has discovered the remains of a far-advanced, long dead civilization. Suddenly, the visitors from Earth are attacked by the same mysterious force that killed the original colonists. This is one of the science fiction classics!

THE CAST: Walter Pidgeon, Anne Francis, Leslie Nielsen, Warren Stevens, Jack Kelly, Richard Anderson, Earl Holliman

Name that movie!

13. An amateur astronomer sights a spaceship which crash lands nearby and buries itself into the ground. Later, he notices that the townspeople seem to be acting strangely and go off into the night on mysterious missions. He learns that the aliens have taken control of these people and are using them to help repair their damaged spaceship. Okay, but it could have been a good deal better.

THE CAST: Richard Carlson, Barbara Rush, Charles Drake, Kathleen Hughes

Name that movie!

14. Mars attacks Earth. All efforts to repel the invaders are futile. When the Martians have nearly destroyed every major city on Earth and are about to complete their conquest, they themselves are all destroyed. It is learned that they had no defense against Earth's native bacteria. Another science fiction classic!

THE CAST: Gene Barry, Ann Robinson, Les Tremayne, Henry Brandon, Jack Kruschen

Name that movie!

15. The last surviving botanical specimens and forests from Earth (after an atomic war) have been placed in huge domes in outer space to avoid their destruction in the poisoned environment. The man in charge of tending these plants and trees is dismayed when he is ordered to forget the whole project, destroy the domes and come home. Two memorable characters (pre-*Star Wars*) are the man's midget robot assistants, Huey and Dewey. It's not *2001: A Space Odyssey,* but it is worth seeing.

THE CAST: Bruce Dern, Cliff Potts, Ron Rifkin, Jesse Vint

Name that movie!

16. Life on Earth is short and sweet in the year 2274. The inhabitants live in domed cities that are run by computers. To keep the population count stable, all citizens are killed on their thirtieth birthday. Those who object to being terminated are hunted down by policemen called Sandmen. One sandman is assigned to find "Sanctuary," the place where runners (those escaping termination) seek refuge. Not a classic, but it could have been one.

THE CAST: Michael York, Jenny Agutter, Richard Jordan, Peter Ustinov

Name that movie!

17. The Americans build a giant defense computer, equipped with self-regulating learning capacities, which controls all automated defenses and weapons. Naturally, the Russians build one too. Suddenly, the two computers develop a mind-link by radio. They decide to take over the world and rule mankind in their own cold, merciless, logical way. This is the ultimate science fiction horror story, in which the "monster" is a "machine." Man has been outsmarted by his own mechanical servant. Well done.

THE CAST: Eric Braeden, Gordon Pinsent, Susan Clark, William Schallert

Name that movie!

18. A scientist discovers that Earth is doomed because the twin planets Zyra and Bellus are moving into our solar system. Bellus will collide with Earth, destroying it, and Zyra will assume its orbit around the Sun. A small group aware of the danger hastily prepares to build a rocketship in an attempt to colonize Zyra before Earth is destroyed. Bellus may be on target, but this film isn't when it comes to solid science fiction entertainment.

THE CAST: Richard Derr, Barbara Rush, Larry Keating, Peter Hanson, John Hoyt

Name that movie!

19. In the year 2022, New York City (and the rest of the world) exists on synthetic foods. There is a terrible overpopulation problem, and the artificial food production cannot meet the demand. Therefore, the government has resorted to using a grisly and secret food extender (recycled human corpses) to cope with the situation. A New York detective discovers this grim truth. An excellent science fiction flick.

THE CAST: Charlton Heston, Edward G. Robinson, Leigh Taylor-Young, Chuck Connors, Brock Peters, Joseph Cotten.

Name that movie!

20. A scientist in England invents a marvelous new clothing fabric which never gets dirty and never wears out. He thinks that this will be a boon to mankind. However, he soon discovers that both labor and management in the textile industry want to suppress his discovery (and jump on his bones). A brilliant science fiction satire that is very funny.

THE CAST: Alec Guinness, Joan Greenwood, Cecil Parker

Name that movie!

True or false?

1. The film *Earth Versus the Flying Saucers* (1956) was based on a book written by Major Donald Keyhoe entitled *Flying Saucers from Outer Space.*

2. *Destination Moon* (1950) was based on the novel *Rocketship Galileo* by Robert A. Heinlein, the famous science fiction writer.

3. In the James Bond movie *Diamonds Are Forever* (1971), a space satellite carrying an atomic death-ray threatens the entire world.

4. "The Blue Danube Waltz" is the background music played in *2001: A Space Odyssey* (1968) as a space shuttle docks with the huge, donut-shaped space station which is slowly rotating on its own axis in Earth's orbit.

5. In *The Day the Earth Caught Fire* (1961), aliens attack with atomic weapons that cause a chain reaction in the Earth's atmosphere.

6. *Fantastic Voyage* (1966) told the story of a spaceflight to an alien planet in another galaxy.

7. *The Conquest of Space* (1955) was a film based on a book titled *Project Mars,* written by the famous rocket scientist Wernher Von Braun.

8. Two of the earliest space travelers in films, Flash Gordon and Buck Rogers, were both played by Buster Crabbe.

9. H. G. Wells, the famous English writer, had several of his works made into movies, including *The Time Machine, First Men in the Moon, The War of the Worlds, Things to Come* and *The Invisible Man.*

10. In *Robinson Crusoe on Mars* (1964), the stranded astronaut's companion was a little monkey.

11. In *Day of the Triffids* (1963), a meteor shower has blinded practically everyone on Earth.

12. *The Incredible Shrinking Man* (1957) told the story of a scientist who experiments with miniaturization and accidentally affects himself instead of the test animal.

13. George Segal starred in *The Terminal Man* (1974).

14. There were three sequels made to *Planet of the Apes* (1968).

15. In *The Time Machine* (1960), the Morlocks were the race in the future who lived underground and could not stand the light of day.

16. The Martians in *The War of the Worlds* (1953) had two large, round eyes and hands with only three fingers.

17. *The Green Slime* (1968) was a remake of *The Blob* (1958).

18. *Wizards* (1976), was a full-length animated science fiction film.

19. In *Demon Seed* (1977), a thinking computer develops a male personality, mates with a woman and fathers a son who is a genius.

20. *Things to Come* (1936), an early but classic science fiction film, starred Raymond Massey, who later played the movie role of Abe Lincoln.

War

Are you ready to move up to the "front lines" of your memory of war movies? As you get going with the questions, you'll begin to hear the deadly chatter of machine guns . . . the drone of bombers overhead . . . the air-raid sirens wailing . . . the thunder of heavy artillery. Get ready to go into action! On land, on the sea and in the air—we're going to put you to the test!

War was an honorable profession back in the early forties, and war movies were then a major film production category. During the forties and fifties, practically every major male film star appeared in one or more war films. It has been said that Hollywood (on film) used more ammunition, killed more people, shot down more planes and sank more ships than were actually accounted for during World War II.

Today, the era of making war films is over—we hope for good, since it takes a war to popularize war films. Of course, we still get an occasional historic-biographic war film *(The Longest Day, Patton, MacArthur)*, but war films no longer constitute a real film category.

You can still catch some of the good old war movies on TV, as they are rerun regularly. There have been some fine stories and some great performances in many a war film. But, aside from the drama and the spectacle of war films, it is worth watching them in order to remind oneself that "war is hell" without having to experience this on a firsthand basis.

Name that star!

1. This popular leading man with rather stoic features made several notable war films. He is best remembered for *The Purple Heart* and *A Walk in the Sun*.

FILM CREDITS: The Purple Heart *(1944)*
Wing and a Prayer *(1944)*
Up in Arms *(1944)*
A Walk in the Sun *(1946)*
The Best Years of Our Lives *(1946)*
The Battle of the Bulge *(1965)*

Name that star!

2. One of Hollywood's greats, he gave distinguished performances (as usual) in some undistinguished war films.

FILM CREDITS: Across the Pacific *(1942)*
Action in the North Atlantic *(1943)*
Sahara *(1943)*
Tokyo Joe *(1949)*
Battle Circus *(1953)*

Name that star!

3. A long-time top star in filmland, he won an Academy Award for his role in *Stalag 17*.

FILM CREDITS: Force of Arms *(1951)*
Submarine Command *(1951)*
Stalag 17 *(1953)*
The Bridges at Toko-Ri *(1954)*
The Proud and the Profane *(1956)*
The Bridge on the River Kwai *(1957)*

Name that star!

4. This pro, who always underacts with great effect, gave us a series of exciting performances in these war flicks.

FILM CREDITS: Gung Ho *(1943)*
Thirty Seconds over Tokyo *(1944)*
The Story of G. I. Joe *(1945)*
Till the End of Time *(1946)*
The Enemy Below *(1957)*
Anzio *(1968)*

Name that star!

5. This Hollywood great gave us some first-rate performances in some memorable war films.

FILM CREDITS: The Immortal Sergeant *(1942)*
Mister Roberts *(1955)*
The Longest Day *(1962)*
The Battle of the Bulge *(1965)*
In Harm's Way *(1965)*
Too Late the Hero *(1969)*

Name that star!

6. One of filmland's top romantic idols, he turned in some entertaining performances in these war vehicles.

FILM CREDITS: The Dawn Patrol *(1938)*
Dive Bomber *(1941)*
Desperate Journey *(1942)*
Edge of Darkness *(1943)*
Northern Pursuit *(1943)*
Objective Burma *(1945)*

Name that star!

7. This great, gutsy star always gave a performance above and beyond the material he was given.

FILM CREDITS: The Fighting 69th *(1940)*
Captains of the Clouds *(1942)*
What Price Glory? *(1952)*
Mister Roberts *(1955)*
The Gallant Hours *(1959)*

Name that star!

8. This tall, raw-boned leading man, though never a top star, really showed his acting mettle in these action-packed war flicks.

FILM CREDITS: Marine Raiders *(1944)*
Flying Leathernecks *(1951)*
Men in War *(1957)*
Battle of the Bulge *(1965)*
The Dirty Dozen *(1967)*
Anzio *(1968)*

Name that star!

9. This lanky, soft-spoken guy is one of Hollywood's top leading men. He usually plays intelligent, serious-minded roles.

FILM CREDITS: Twelve O'Clock High *(1949)*
The Purple Plain *(1955)*
Pork Chop Hill *(1959)*
On the Beach *(1959)*
The Guns of Navarone *(1961)*
MacArthur *(1977)*

Name that star!

10. A rugged, handsome actor, this star has most often been seen in westerns. However, he seemed quite at home in action-war films.

FILM CREDITS: Paris Calling *(1941)*
To the Shores of Tripoli *(1942)*
Bombardier *(1943)*
Corvette K-225 *(1943)*
Gung Ho *(1943)*
China Sky *(1944)*

Name that star!

11. This Hollywood legend could be remembered just for his performances in a large number of "good" war movies. However, these movies represent only a portion of his long list of film credits.

FILM CREDITS: Back to Bataan *(1944)*
They Were Expendable *(1945)*
Sands of Iwo Jima *(1949)*
Flying Leathernecks *(1951)*
In Harm's Way *(1965)*
Cast a Giant Shadow *(1966)*

Name that star!

12. This fair-haired leading man played in detective-gangster films and westerns, and he chalked up these war-film credits too.

FILM CREDITS: Halls of Montezuma *(1950)*
Destination Gobi *(1953)*
Take the High Ground *(1953)*
Time Limit *(1957)*
The Bedford Incident *(1965)*

Name that star!

13. This "bird" (that's a clue to his name) is a tall, handsome, gentlemanly actor. He has played in a wide variety of films and turned in a "flock" of fine performances.

FILM CREDITS: Flight Command *(1940)*
Command Decision *(1948)*
Men of the Fighting Lady *(1954)*

Name that star!

14. One of filmdom's tough guys, he turned in his usual taut, gripping performances in these notable films.

FILM CREDITS: From Here to Eternity *(1953)*
Run Silent, Run Deep *(1958)*
Castle Keep *(1969)*

Name that star!

15. This very popular, suave English star was at the top of his form in *The Desert Fox.* Remember?

FILM CREDITS: Secret Mission *(1942)*
The Desert Fox *(1951)*
The Desert Rats *(1953)*
Torpedo Bay *(1964)*
The Blue Max *(1966)*

Name that star!

16. A robust, athletic star, he appeared in many epics, and despite the cute dimple on his chin he always made a war film worth the price of admission.

FILM CREDITS: Paths of Glory *(1957)*
Seven Days in May *(1964)*
In Harm's Way *(1965)*
Heroes of Telemark *(1965)*
Cast a Giant Shadow *(1966)*
Is Paris Burning? *(1966)*

Name that star!

17. One of Hollywood's most versatile top stars, he won an Academy Award for his supporting role in *From Here to Eternity.*

FILM CREDITS: From Here to Eternity *(1953)*
Kings Go Forth *(1958)*
Never So Few *(1959)*
None But the Brave *(1965)*
Von Ryan's Express *(1965)*
Cast a Giant Shadow *(1966)*

Name that star!

18. He was not a big star, yet he always turned in a solid performance. He had a nasal, but very pleasant speaking voice and usually played a hard-nosed officer.

FILM CREDITS: Home of the Brave *(1949)*
Force of Arms *(1951)*
Retreat Hell *(1952)*
Beachhead *(1954)*
Strategic Air Command *(1955)*

Name that star!

19. It takes more than freckles and blond hair to make a movie star. It takes talent and charisma—and this fellow has both.

FILM CREDITS: Thirty Seconds Over Tokyo *(1944)*
Battleground *(1950)*
The Caine Mutiny *(1954)*
Go for Broke *(1957)*
Battle Squadron *(1969)*

Name that star!

20. One of the all-time greats of the screen, this tall, lanky guy did more acting with his pauses between lines than his fellow players did when they were speaking their lines. He won an Academy Award for his role in *Sergeant York.*

FILM CREDITS: A Farewell to Arms *(1932)*
Sergeant York *(1941)*
For Whom the Bell Tolls *(1943)*
Cloak and Dagger *(1946)*
Task Force *(1949)*
The Court Martial of Billy Mitchell *(1955)*

Name that star!

Name that star!

Multiple choice

1. *Above and Beyond* (1952), the film version of the dropping of the atomic bomb on Hiroshima, starred_____?
a. Robert Young b. Robert Taylor c. Gregory Peck
d. Clark Gable e. Robert Montgomery

2. Who starred in *To Hell and Back* (1955)?
a. Steve McQueen b. Roger Moore c. Audie Murphy
d. Lee Marvin e. Lloyd Bridges

3. Who co-starred with Eddie Albert in *Attack* (1956), a story about the Battle of the Bulge?
a. Jack Palance b. Glenn Ford c. Frank
Lovejoy d. Edmond O'Brien e. Dana Andrews

4. Name the actor who starred with George C. Scott in *Patton* (1969).
a. Rod Steiger b. Cliff Robertson c. Karl
Malden d. Gene Hackman e. Henry Fonda

5. Who starred with William Holden in *The Bridges at Toko-Ri* (1954)?
a. Mickey Rooney b. Jeff Chandler c. Robert Ryan
d. Alec Guinness e. Warren Beatty

6. Name the actress who also starred in *The Bridges at Toko-Ri* (1954).
a. Deborah Kerr b. Grace Kelly c. Sally Field
d. Julie Andrews e. Nancy Kwan

7. Name the star of *Destination Tokyo* (1943), a story about submarine warfare in the Pacific.
a. Clark Gable b. Spencer Tracy c. James Stewart
d. Cary Grant e. Robert Taylor

8. Who starred in *Air Force* (1943)?
a. James Stewart   **b.** John Wayne   **c.** William Holden
d. John Garfield   **e.** Alan Ladd

9. Who played the role of the nurse who fell in love with Humphrey Bogart in *Battle Circus* (1952)?
a. Julie London   **b.** Joan Fontaine   **c.** Barbara Stanwyck
d. Celeste Holm   **e.** June Allyson

10. In the film *The Bridge at Remagen* (1969), who played the German major trying to hold the bridge against the Allies?
a. Robert Shaw   **b.** Curt Jurgens   **c.** James Mason   **d.** Robert Vaughn   **e.** Helmut Dantine

11. Name the star of *Catch 22* (1970).
a. Alan Alda   **b.** Larry Hagman   **c.** Alan Arkin   **d.** Donald Sutherland   **e.** Gene Wilder

12. Who starred with Donald Sutherland in the film *M*A*S*H* (1970)?
a. Alan Alda   **b.** Aldo Ray   **c.** Warren Beatty   **d.** Lee Marvin   **e.** Elliott Gould

13. *Kelly's Heroes* (1970) starred_____?
a. Dana Andrews   **b.** Dane Clark   **c.** Clint Eastwood
d. Charles Bronson   **e.** Robert Redford

14. Who starred with George Peppard in *Tobruk* (1967)?
a. Gregory Peck   **b.** Kirk Douglas   **c.** Marlon Brando
d. Rock Hudson   **e.** Burt Lancaster

15. MacDonald Carey and Robert Preston were featured players in *Wake Island* (1942), but who was the star?
a. John Wayne   **b.** Pat O'Brien   **c.** Brian Donlevy   **d.** Ward Bond   **e.** Randolph Scott

16. Who was the star of *Strategic Air Command* (1955)?
a. Clark Gable **b.** James Stewart **c.** John Wayne **d.** Gary Cooper **e.** Robert Ryan

17. Who played the title role in *The Court Martial of Billy Mitchell* (1955)?
a. Henry Fonda **b.** James Cagney **c.** Gary Cooper **d.** James Stewart **e.** Fred MacMurray

18. Who played the role of the general who tried to take over the country in *Seven Days in May* (1964)?
a. Kirk Douglas **b.** Burt Lancaster **c.** Lee Marvin **d.** Spencer Tracy **e.** Gene Hackman

19. *The Guns of Navarone* (1961) starred Gregory Peck and a popular English star. What was his name?
a. James Mason **b.** David Niven **c.** Brian Aherne **d.** Michael Caine **e.** Roger Moore

20. Who was the star of *Crash Dive* (1943), the submarine adventure story of World War II?
a. Dane Clark **b.** Henry Fonda **c.** Tyrone Power **d.** John Wayne **e.** Cary Grant

21. *The Cruel Sea* (1952), a World War II drama, starred _____?
a. John Mills **b.** Jack Hawkins **c.** Alec Guinness **d.** David Niven **e.** Burt Lancaster

22. Who starred in *Darby's Rangers* (1957), the story of an American commando unit in Britain?
a. James Garner **b.** Randolph Scott **c.** John Wayne **d.** Lee Marvin **e.** Robert Ryan

23. *Dunkirk* (1958), the story of the British rescue evacuation from the Allied disaster in Normandy, starred _____?
a. Walter Pidgeon **b.** John Mills **c.** Richard Attenborough **d.** Ralph Bellamy **e.** John Gregson

24. Allied prisoners plan an escape from a German POW camp in *The Great Escape* (1963). Who co-starred in this film with James Garner?
a. Jack Palance **b.** Charles Bronson **c.** Karl Malden
d. Steve McQueen **e.** Cliff Robertson

25. A good action-war film, *Guadalcanal Diary* (1943), had a fine cast—Lloyd Nolan, William Bendix, Richard Conte, Anthony Quinn, Richard Jaeckel, etc.—but who starred?
a. John Wayne **b.** Errol Flynn **c.** Brian Donlevy **d.** John Payne **e.** Preston Foster

26. *O.S.S.* (1946) told the story of American spies parachuted into France in '43. Who starred?
a. Richard Conte **b.** Frank Lovejoy **c.** Dennis O'Keefe
d. Edmond O'Brien **e.** Alan Ladd

27. *Operation Crossbow* (1965) was an action-packed World War II spy film. Name the star.
a. George Peppard **b.** Rock Hudson **c.** Kirk Douglas
d. Robert Wagner **e.** Richard Widmark

28. The story about supplying Patton's army from the Normandy beachhead was told in *Red Ball Express* (1952). Who starred?
a. Lloyd Nolan **b.** Van Johnson **c.** Steve McQueen
d. Burt Lancaster **e.** Jeff Chandler

29. *So Proudly We Hail* (1943) was a war story about Army nurses in the Pacific. Which one of these actresses starred?
a. Irene Dunne **b.** Anne Baxter **c.** Claudette Colbert
d. Claire Trevor **e.** Myrna Loy

30. An American sub destroys a Japanese carrier in Tokyo Bay in *Torpedo Run* (1958). Who starred?
a. Glenn Ford **b.** Cary Grant **c.** Robert Taylor **d.** Burt Lancaster **e.** Fred MacMurray

31. *Up from the Beach* (1965) was a film about the landing at Normandy. Name the actor who starred.
a. Don Murray   **b.** Cliff Robertson   **c.** Vic Morrow
d. James Coburn   **e.** Robert Culp

32. Who starred in *The War Lover* (1962)?
a. Lee Marvin   **b.** Audie Murphy   **c.** Charles Bronson
d. Anthony Quinn   **e.** Steve McQueen

33. A film story about U.S. bomber pilots in the Pacific during World War II was called *The Wild Blue Yonder* (1952). Who starred?
a. Wendell Corey   **b.** William Holden   **c.** Glenn Ford
d. Gregory Peck   **e.** Clark Gable

34. One of the best war films about Air Force pilots, *Winged Victory* (1944), starred_____?
a. Dennis Morgan   **b.** Lon McCallister   **c.** Dana Andrews
d. Douglas Fairbanks, Jr.   **e.** Tyrone Power

35. *All the Young Men* (1960) was the story of a Marine patrol in Korea commanded by a black man. Who co-starred with Sidney Poitier?
a. Alan Ladd   **b.** Frank Sinatra   **c.** Charlton
Heston   **d.** Robert Sterling   **e.** Joseph Cotten

36. Who starred in *Back to Bataan* (1945)?
a. James Cagney   **b.** John Wayne   **c.** Randolph Scott
d. Clark Gable   **e.** Spencer Tracy

37. *Captain Eddie* (1945), a story about World War I flying ace Eddie Rickenbacker, starred _____?
a. Fred MacMurray   **b.** James Stewart   **c.** Gregory Peck
d. Gary Cooper   **e.** Fredric March

38. Who starred in *Cockleshell Heroes* (1955)?
a. Tyrone Power   **b.** Gig Young   **c.** Stewart Granger
d. Jose Ferrer   **e.** Yul Brynner

39. *I Was Monty's Double* (1958) starred which one of these actors?
a. Alec Guinness   **b.** Michael Rennie   **c.** John Mills   **d.** David Niven   **e.** Robert Newton

40. Who starred with Tina Louise and Burt Reynolds in *Armored Command* (1961)?
a. Jack Palance   **b.** Eddie Albert   **c.** Victor Mature
d. Howard Keel   **e.** George C. Scott

Name that movie!

1. A group of survivors from a torpedoed passenger ship find themselves adrift at sea along with the German U-boat commander who was responsible for sinking their ship. A one-set classic!

THE CAST: Tallulah Bankhead, Walter Slezak, Henry Hull, John Hodiak, Canada Lee, William Bendix, Mary Anderson, Heather Angel

Name that movie!

2. The Allied landing at Normandy in 1944 with an all-star cast. An epic war movie almost as big as the real thing.

THE CAST: John Wayne, Robert Mitchum, Henry Fonda, Robert Ryan, Rod Steiger, Peter Lawford, Robert Wagner, Paul Anka, Fabian, Tommy Sands, Richard Beymer, Mel Ferrer, Jeffrey Hunter, Sal Mineo, Roddy McDowall, Stuart Whitman, Steve Forrest, Eddie Albert, Red Buttons, Edmond O'Brien, Tom Tryon, plus many more

Name that movie!

3. Field Marshal Rommel returns to Germany after his North African campaign. Upset over his defeat and disillusioned with Hitler's regime, he becomes involved in the July plot against Hitler. Well done, interesting and memorable.

THE CAST: James Mason, Jessica Tandy, Cedric Hardwicke, Luther Adler, Everett Sloane, Leo G. Carroll, George Macready, Richard Boone, Edward Franz

Name that movie!

4. This is the story of a group of American prisoners of war in Japan who are tried and executed. Grim and gripping.

THE CAST: Dana Andrews, Richard Conte, Farley Granger, Kevin O'Shea, Sam Levene, Don Barry, Richard Loo, Tala Birell

Name that movie!

5. The story of a day in the life of an infantry patrol during the Salerno campaign in 1943. A suspenseful, vivid picture of the reality of combat as the foot soldiers have to face it—great!

THE CAST: Dana Andrews, Richard Conte, Sterling Holloway, John Ireland, Lloyd Bridges, Huntz Hall

Name that movie!

6. This war film was based on a famous novel by James Jones. It tells the story of life in a Honolulu barrack at the time of the attack on Pearl Harbor. Powerful—a major movie of its kind. Sinatra won an Academy Award for his performance.

THE CAST: Burt Lancaster, Deborah Kerr, Frank Sinatra, Donna Reed, Ernest Borgnine, Montgomery Clift

Name that movie!

7. The Allied juggernaut in Europe (the Ardennes) runs into a major snag as a crack Nazi panzer force puts up a tough battle. A fine war epic with an excellent cast. Memorable.

THE CAST: Henry Fonda, Robert Shaw, Robert Ryan, Telly Savalas, Dana Andrews, George Montgomery, Ty Hardin, Pier Angeli, Charles Bronson, James MacArthur

Name that movie!

8. The story of Colonel Doolittle's planning and execution of the first American bomb raid on the Japanese mainland. This one ranks among the best World War II films ever made. First rate!

THE CAST: Spencer Tracy, Van Johnson, Robert Walker, Phyllis Thaxter, Tim Murdock, Don Defore, Robert Mitchum

Name that movie!

9. This navy war film highlighted some of the episodes in the career of Admiral William F. (Bull) Halsey during World War II. Cagney is always worth watching.

THE CAST: James Cagney, Dennis Weaver, Richard Jaeckel, Ward Costello

Name that movie!

10. A World War II story of the aerial bombardment of Germany, it highlighted some of the tough behind-the-scenes decisions that had to be hammered out by the top brass. A well-done war epic with a big and talented cast.

THE CAST: Clark Gable, Walter Pidgeon, Van Johnson, Brian Donlevy, John Hodiak, Charles Bickford, Edward Arnold, Marshall Thompson, Richard Quine, Cameron Mitchell, Warner Anderson, John McIntire

Name that movie!

11. This is the story of the U.S. Navy's counterattack against the Japanese after Pearl Harbor. Considering its huge, stellar cast, it should have been a real classic. Unfortunately, it misses that mark by a wide margin.

THE CAST: John Wayne, Kirk Douglas, Patricia Neal, Tom Tryon, Paula Prentiss, Brandon de Wilde, Stanley Holloway, Burgess Meredith, Henry Fonda, Dana Andrews, Franchot Tone, Jill Haworth, George Kennedy, Hugh O'Brian, Carroll O'Connor, Patrick O'Neal, Slim Pickens, Bruce Cabot, Larry Hagman, James Mitchum

Name that movie!

12. This is the story of a World War I German ace and his postwar involvement with his superior officer. Terrific flying sequences and well done all around.

THE CAST: George Peppard, James Mason, Ursula Andress, Jeremy Kemp

Name that movie!

13. The true life story of an easy-going American hillbilly who became a World War I hero. An excellent cast—Cooper is colossal!

THE CAST: Gary Cooper, Joan Leslie, Walter Brennan, George Tobias, David Bruce, Stanley Ridges, Margaret Wycherly, Dickie Moore, Ward Bond, June Lockhart

Name that movie!

14. A news reporter (they called them war correspondents in those days) joins an Allied task force preparing for a landing in Italy. A fine cast without anything interesting to say. Clue: Where they land in Italy is the title of the picture.

THE CAST: Robert Mitchum, Peter Falk, Arthur Kennedy, Robert Ryan, Earl Holliman, Mark Damon, Anthony Steel, Patrick Magee

Name that movie!

15. A war-hardened sergeant inspires a group of raw recruits under his command in the North African campaign before he is killed in action. Well-done drama that belongs on any list of war films worth remembering.

THE CAST: Henry Fonda, Thomas Mitchell, Maureen O'Hara, Allyn Joslyn, Reginald Gardiner, Melville Cooper

Name that movie!

16. In 1947, an American ex-military man goes to Israel to help in the fight against the Arabs. A fine war epic that stops just this side of being absolutely great.

THE CAST: Kirk Douglas, Angie Dickinson, Senta Berger, Luther Adler, Stathis Giallelis, Chaim Topol, John Wayne, Frank Sinatra, Yul Brynner, Gary Merrill

Name that movie!

17. Some American flyers battle the Japanese in China during World War II. (Clue: After the war, some of these pilots formed an air cargo line using the nickname they inherited from their China war days.) Not much here beyond John Wayne, but for most of us that's always enough.

THE CAST: John Wayne, John Carroll, Anna Lee, Paul Kelly, Mae Clarke

Name that movie!

18. A U.S. Air Force general, who is not playing with a full deck, launches a nuclear attack on Russia. Recall attempts fail, retaliation is certain, and all involved await the destruction of civilization. Wild, woolly and wonderful!

THE CAST: Peter Sellers, George C. Scott, Peter Bull, Sterling Hayden, Keenan Wynn, Slim Pickens, James Earl Jones

Name that movie!

19. During World War II, twelve army convicts serving life sentences are recruited for a suicide commando mission. Taut and terrific—it's a classic!

THE CAST: Lee Marvin, Ernest Borgnine, Robert Ryan, Charles Bronson, John Cassavettes, Ralph Meeker, Clint Walker, Robert Webber, Donald Sutherland

Name that movie!

20. During World War II, an American captain leads an escape of English prisoners of war from an Italian POW camp. They capture a train and head for the Swiss Alps. An action-thriller!

THE CAST: Frank Sinatra, Trevor Howard, Sergio Fantoni, Edward Mulhare, Brad Dexter, John Leyton, James Brolin, Adolfo Celi

Name that movie!

True or false?

1. One of the stars of *In Harm's Way* (1965) was Carroll O'Connor (of Archie Bunker fame).

2. Comedian Don Rickles was one of the stars of *Kelly's Heroes* (1970).

3. Four actors who played the role of Hitler in films were: Charlie Chaplin in *The Great Dictator* (1940); Luther Adler in *The Magic Face* (1951); Richard Basehart in *Hitler* (1963); Alec Guinness in *Hitler: The Last Ten Days* (1973).

4. *PT 109* (1963), the story of President Kennedy's wartime experiences, starred Dale Robertson.

5. The actress who played the title role in *Mrs. Miniver* (1942) was Barbara Stanwyck.

6. *The Bridge on the River Kwai* starred Alec Guinness.

7. No war movie ever won an Academy Award for Best Picture.

8. A submarine war thriller called *Destination Tokyo* (1943) starred Cary Grant as the sub commander.

9. Edward G. Robinson never made a war movie.

10. *The Beginning or the End* (1947) was a film about American scientists who were working to perfect the atomic bomb for use in World War II.

11. *They Were Expendable* (1945), which starred John Wayne and Robert Montgomery, was a story about torpedo boats in action in the Pacific during World War II.

12. *13 Rue Madeleine* (1946) was a war spy story and starred James Cagney.

13. John Wayne, not John Payne, starred with Maureen O'Hara in *To the Shores of Tripoli* (1942).

14. *Hell in the Pacific* (1969) was a war film about the battle of Wake Island.

15. Tony Curtis and Frank Sinatra once starred together in a war melodrama called *Kings Go Forth* (1958).

16. Joan Crawford starred in *Reunion in France* (1943), the story of a Paris dress designer who helps an American flyer during World War II. Her co-star in this picture was Clark Gable.

17. *Mister Roberts* (1955) starred Henry Fonda and James Cagney. But it was Jack Lemmon who won an Academy Award for his role in this film.

18. Norman Mailer's big war novel, *The Naked and the Dead,* was made into a movie in 1958 and starred Aldo Ray.

19. One of the stars of *Paths of Glory* (1957) was Adolph Menjou, the great character actor.

20. *The Young Lions* (1958) starred Montgomery Clift, Marlon Brando, *and* Dean Martin!

Adventure-Suspense -Thrillers

NAME THAT STAR!

1. James Stewart
2. Cary Grant
3. Errol Flynn
4. Gary Cooper
5. Ray Milland
6. Tyrone Power
7. Joseph Cotten
8. Gregory Peck
9. Susan Hayward
10. Rita Hayworth
11. Maureen O'Hara
12. Barbara Stanwyck
13. Janet Leigh
14. Burt Lancaster
15. Alan Ladd
16. Robert Taylor
17. Clark Gable
18. Douglas Fairbanks, Jr.
19. Kirk Douglas
20. Charlton Heston

NAME THAT STAR! multiple choice

1. a	11. a	21. b	31. d
2. c	12. a	22. a	32. e
3. d	13. b	23. b	33. c
4. a	14. a	24. c	34. a
5. b	15. c	25. c	35. b
6. a	16. d	26. b	36. d
7. e	17. c	27. d	37. b
8. b	18. a	28. c	38. e
9. e	19. b	29. c	39. a
10. c	20. d	30. a	40. b

NAME THAT MOVIE!

1. Fail Safe *(1964)*
2. The Manchurian Candidate *(1962)*
3. Rear Window *(1954)*
4. Between Two Worlds *(1944)*
5. The Man Who Would Be King *(1975)*
6. The Adventures of Robin Hood *(1938)*
7. Seven Days to Noon *(1950)*
8. The Set-Up *(1949)*
9. Shadow of a Doubt *(1943)*
10. The Seventh Cross *(1944)*
11. The Seventh Voyage of Sinbad *(1958)*
12. Tom Jones *(1963)*
13. The Two Mrs. Carrolls *(1945)*
14. Goldfinger *(1964)*
15. Shake Hands with the Devil *(1959)*
16. The Blue Dahlia *(1946)*
17. The Black Swan *(1942)*
18. The Hot Rock *(1972)*
19. Lost Horizon *(1937)*
20. Spellbound *(1945)*

TRUE OR FALSE?

1. True
2. False—Richard Burton starred.
3. False—Heston starred only in *Airport '75* (1974).
4. True
5. False—It was a political drama about the IRA.
6. True
7. True
8. True
9. True
10. False—Edward G. Robinson starred.
11. True
12. True
13. True
14. True
15. False—Robert Ryan played Captain Nemo.
16. False—Joseph Cotten starred with Welles.
17. True
18. False—Robert Wagner played the lead.
19. True
20. True

Musicals

NAME THAT STAR! male

1. James Cagney
2. Ray Bolger
3. Dick Powell
4. Fred Astaire
5. Donald O'Connor
6. Gene Kelly
7. Dan Dailey
8. Maurice Chevalier
9. Bing Crosby
10. Buddy Ebsen
11. Frank Sinatra
12. Eddie Cantor
13. Van Johnson
14. Danny Kaye
15. Mickey Rooney
16. Dean Martin
17. Oscar Levant
18. Sammy Davis, Jr.
19. George Murphy
20. Gordon MacRae

NAME THAT STAR! female

1. Judy Garland
2. Vera-Ellen
3. Doris Day
4. Deanna Durbin
5. Rita Hayworth
6. Ginger Rogers
7. Kathryn Grayson
8. Alice Faye
9. Betty Grable
10. Betty Hutton
11. Cyd Charisse
12. Ann Miller
13. Debbie Reynolds
14. Lena Horne
15. Carmen Miranda
16. Shirley Jones
17. Ethel Merman
18. Esther Williams
19. Leslie Caron
20. Jeanette MacDonald

NAME THAT STAR! multiple choice

1. a	6. d	11. e	16. d
2. b	7. e	12. e	17. b
3. b	8. a	13. c	18. a
4. b	9. b	14. b	19. d
5. d	10. a	15. b	20. c

NAME THAT MOVIE!

1. Calamity Jane *(1953)*
2. Camelot *(1967)*
3. Can Can *(1960)*
4. Doctor Dolittle *(1967)*
5. Easter Parade *(1948)*
6. Hans Christian Andersen *(1952)*
7. The Helen Morgan Story *(1957)*
8. Holiday Inn *(1942)*
9. I'll See You in My Dreams *(1951)*
10. Kismet *(1955)*
11. Kiss Me Kate *(1953)*
12. Night and Day *(1945)*
13. On the Town *(1949)*
14. Paint Your Wagon *(1969)*
15. Rhapsody in Blue *(1945)*
16. Tea for Two *(1950)*
17. Singin' in the Rain *(1952)*
18. Yankee Doodle Dandy *(1942)*
19. Words and Music *(1948)*
20. White Christmas *(1954)*

TRUE OR FALSE?

1. True
2. False—Gene Kelly starred.
3. False—Barbra Streisand played the title role.
4. False—Astaire and Kelly appeared together in *Ziegfeld Follies* (1946).
5. True
6. False—Rosalind Russell co-starred.
7. True
8. False—It was Paul Whiteman.
9. False—Liberace appeared in *Footlight Varieties* (1951), *Sincerely Yours* (1955) and *Girl Crazy* (1966).
10. False—Bing Crosby and Mary Martin starred.
11. True
12. False—Larry Parks starred.
13. False—Ray Bolger was the dancer this time.
14. True
15. True
16. True
17. False—Petula Clark starred.
18. False—Deborah Kerr played the female lead.
19. False—Christopher Plummer co-starred.
20. True

Gangster-Detective

NAME THAT STAR!

1. Robert Ryan
2. James Cagney
3. Edward G. Robinson
4. Richard Conte
5. Victor Mature
6. Robert Mitchum
7. Glenn Ford
8. George Raft
9. Humphrey Bogart
10. Alan Ladd

11. Dana Andrews
12. Ida Lupino
13. Burt Lancaster
14. Frank Sinatra
15. Lee J. Cobb
16. Charles McGraw
17. Gloria Grahame
18. Richard Widmark
19. George Sanders
20. William Bendix

NAME THAT STAR! multiple choice

1. b	11. a	21. d	31. b
2. a	12. d	22. a	32. d
3. c	13. c	23. a	33. b
4. c	14. c	24. b	34. b
5. a	15. c	25. a	35. c
6. a	16. a	26. e	36. a
7. b	17. c	27. b	37. a
8. b	18. d	28. c	38. b
9. b	19. d	29. a	39. a
10. c	20. d	30. b	40. b

NAME THAT MOVIE!

1. Laura *(1944)*
2. On the Waterfront *(1954)*
3. Murder by Death *(1976)*
4. This Gun for Hire *(1942)*
5. Dead Reckoning *(1947)*
6. The Big Heat *(1953)*
7. Bonnie and Clyde *(1967)*
8. Charley Varrick *(1973)*

9. Birdman of Alcatraz *(1962)*
10. Key Largo *(1948)*
11. Boomerang *(1947)*
12. Sorry, Wrong Number *(1948)*
13. Cops and Robbers *(1973)*
14. Double Indemnity *(1944)*
15. The Enforcer *(1950)*

16. Dirty Harry *(1971)*
17. Death Wish *(1974)*
18. Bloody Mama *(1971)*

19. The Sting *(1973)*
20. The French Connection *(1971)*

TRUE OR FALSE?

1. True
2. True
3. False—His name was Sam Spade.
4. True
5. False—Peter Cushing played the master sleuth.
6. False—William Powell starred with Myrna Loy.
7. False
8. True
9. True
10. True
11. False—George Montgomery played Marlowe.
12. True

13. False—Full-length Dick Tracy films include *Dick Tracy* (1945), *Dick Tracy vs. Cueball* (1946), *Dick Tracy Meets Gruesome* (1947) and *Dick Tracy's Dilemma* (1947).
14. True—*Brother Orchid* (1940) was the title.
15. True
16. True
17. True
18. True
19. True
20. False—Mary Astor played the female lead.

Westerns

NAME THAT STAR!

1. William Holden
2. Gregory Peck
3. Burt Lancaster
4. Richard Widmark
5. James Stewart
6. Randolph Scott
7. Anthony Quinn
8. Robert Mitchum
9. Lee Marvin
10. Joel McCrea
11. Charlton Heston
12. Glenn Ford
13. Henry Fonda
14. Kirk Douglas
15. Ernest Borgnine
16. Rock Hudson
17. Jack Palance
18. Robert Ryan
19. Clint Eastwood
20. Charles Bronson

NAME THAT STAR! multiple choice

1. d	11. c	21. b	31. c
2. d	12. e	22. a	32. e
3. a	13. a	23. c	33. b
4. d	14. e	24. e	34. c
5. d	15. c	25. c	35. a
6. b	16. b	26. b	36. a
7. e	17. b	27. a	37. a
8. b	18. d	28. b	38. b
9. c	19. a	29. a	39. e
10. e	20. c	30. b	40. c

NAME THAT MOVIE!

1. The Magnificent Seven *(1960)*
2. Billy Jack *(1971)*
3. Cheyenne Autumn *(1964)*
4. A Big Hand for the Little Lady *(1966)*
5. High Noon *(1952)*
6. The Treasure of Sierra Madre *(1948)*
7. Destry Rides Again *(1939)*
8. The Ox-Bow Incident *(1942)*
9. Pony Express *(1953)*
10. The Professionals *(1966)*
11. 3:10 to Yuma *(1957)*
12. Butch Cassidy and the Sundance Kid *(1969)*
13. She Wore a Yellow Ribbon *(1949)*
14. Red River *(1948)*

15. My Darling Clementine *(1946)*
16. The Searchers *(1956)*
17. The Big Country *(1958)*
18. Hondo *(1954)*
19. A Gunfight *(1970)*
20. Drums Along the Mohawk *(1939)*

TRUE OR FALSE?

1. False—Robert Redford starred.
2. True
3. False—Stewart and Wayne starred together in *The Man Who Shot Liberty Valance* (1962) and *The Shootist* (1976).
4. True—Holden and Wayne appeared together in *The Horse Soldiers* (1959).
5. True
6. False—Hudson and Wayne starred together in *The Undefeated* (1969).
7. False—Robinson appeared in *Cheyenne Autumn* (1964) and *Mackenna's Gold* (1968).
8. True
9. True—Douglas and Wayne appeared together in *The War Wagon* (1969).
10. False—*Cimarron* (1931) won the Best Picture award.
11. False—Lemmon starred in *The Cowboy* (1957) with Glenn Ford.
12. True—Bronson and Fonda appeared together in *Once Upon a Time in the West* (1969).
13. False—Gable appeared in a number of westerns: *Honky Tonk* (1941), *Across the Wide Missouri* (1951), *Lone Star* (1952), *The Tall Men* (1955), *The King and Four Queens* (1956) and *The Misfits* (1960).
14. False—Brynner appeared in several other westerns: *Invitation to a Gunfighter* (1964), *The Long Duel* (1967), *Villa Rides* (1968) and *Catlow* (1972).
15. False—Ben Johnson starred.
16. True
17. False—Presley starred in *Charro* (1969).
18. False—Wayne and Fonda appeared together in two westerns, *Fort Apache* (1948) and *How the West Was Won* (1962).
19. True
20. True

Horror

NAME THAT STAR!

1. Vincent Price
2. Peter Cushing
3. John Carradine
4. Lon Chaney, Jr.
5. Christopher Lee
6. Peter Lorre
7. George Zucco
8. Barbara Shelley
9. Basil Rathbone
10. Herbert Lom
11. Conrad Veidt
12. Ray Milland
13. Lionel Atwill
14. Tom Conway
15. E. E. Clive
16. Bela Lugosi
17. Boris Karloff
18. J. Carrol Naish
19. Hazel Court
20. Barbara Steele

NAME THAT STAR! multiple choice

1. a
2. c
3. a
4. c
5. e
6. a
7. b
8. a
9. b
10. a
11. a
12. d
13. d
14. a
15. b
16. b
17. a
18. c
19. a
20. b
21. c
22. a
23. d
24. a
25. a
26. e
27. d
28. a
29. b
30. b
31. c
32. c
33. b
34. a
35. e
36. a
37. c
38. b
39. c
40. a

NAME THAT MOVIE!

1. House of Wax *(1953)*
2. Attack of the Crab Monsters *(1957)*
3. Ben *(1972)*
4. The Cat People *(1942)*
5. The Creature from the Black Lagoon *(1954)*
6. The Abominable Dr. Phibes *(1971)*
7. Rosemary's Baby *(1969)*
8. The Exorcist *(1973)*
9. The Body Snatcher *(1945)*
10. The Beast with Five Fingers *(1946)*

11. The Bride of Frankenstein (1935)
12. Curse of the Demon (1958)
13. Dr. Terror's House of Horrors (1965)
14. Dracula (1930)
15. Frogs (1972)

16. The Fly (1958)
17. The Mummy (1932)
18. The Phantom of the Opera (1925)
19. The Invisible Man (1933)
20. Tales from the Crypt (1972)

TRUE OR FALSE?

1. True
2. True
3. True—Abbott and Costello Meet Dr. Jekyll and Mr. Hyde (1953) co-starred Karloff and Abbott and Costello Meet Frankenstein (1948) co-starred Lugosi.
4. True
5. True
6. False—Son of Kong (1935) was the sequel.
7. False
8. True
9. True
10. True—Denning appeared in The Creature with the Atomic Brain (1955), The Creature from the Black Lagoon (1954) and The Black Scorpion (1957).

11. True
12. True
13. False—Ralph Bellamy played the doctor.
14. True
15. False—Lon Chaney, Bela Lugosi and Glenn Strange all played the role of Frankenstein in films.
16. False—Blood Alley (1955) was a John Wayne film.
17. False—Christopher Lee starred in the 1959 version.
18. True
19. False—Night People (1954), starring Gregory Peck, was about the Cold War in Berlin.
20. True

Comedies

NAME THAT STAR!

1. Jack Lemmon
2. Alec Guinness
3. Cary Grant
4. Gary Cooper
5. Doris Day
6. Katharine Hepburn
7. Jerry Lewis
8. Tony Randall
9. Peter Sellers
10. Bob Hope
11. Carole Lombard
12. Claudette Colbert
13. Rosalind Russell
14. Jean Arthur
15. Ginger Rogers
16. Charles Coburn
17. David Niven
18. Myrna Loy
19. James Stewart
20. Jack Benny

NAME THAT STAR! multiple choice

1. b	11. e	21. a	31. d
2. a	12. a	22. a	32. a
3. c	13. d	23. a	33. b
4. e	14. b	24. d	34. c
5. b	15. a	25. b	35. c
6. c	16. c	26. c	36. c
7. b	17. b	27. a	37. b
8. c	18. e	28. b	38. e
9. d	19. c	29. b	39. c
10. c	20. c	30. b	40. d

NAME THAT MOVIE!

1. The Horn Blows at Midnight *(1945)*
2. Monkey Business *(1952)*
3. Champagne for Caesar *(1950)*
4. His Girl Friday *(1940)*
5. It's a Mad, Mad, Mad, Mad World *(1963)*
6. I Love You Alice B. Toklas *(1968)*
7. The Apartment *(1960)*
8. Arsenic and Old Lace *(1942)*
9. Kind Hearts and Coronets *(1949)*
10. The Producers *(1967)*

11. How to Murder Your Wife *(1965)*
12. The Fortune Cookie *(1966)*
13. The Seven Year Itch *(1955)*
14. Bell, Book and Candle *(1958)*
15. The Pink Panther *(1963)*
16. The Lavender Hill Mob *(1951)*
17. Move Over Darling *(1963)*
18. Born Yesterday *(1950)*
19. A Day at the Races *(1937)*
20. Adam's Rib *(1949)*

TRUE OR FALSE?

1. True
2. False—Groucho appeared in five films alone, including *Copacabana* (1947) and *Double Dynamite* (1951).
3. False—Berle has appeared in more than a dozen films, including one based upon his autobiography *Always Leave Them Laughing* (1949).
4. False—Costello made a film alone called *The Thirty-Foot Bride of Candy Rock* (1959).
5. True
6. False—Allen made several films: *Thanks a Million* (1935), *Love Thy Neighbor* (1941), *It's in the Bag* (1945), *We're Not Married* (1952) and *Full House* (1953).
7. True
8. True—Lamarr appeared with Stewart in *Come Live with Me* (1941); Dietrich appeared with him in *Destry Rides Again* (1939).
9. True
10. True
11. True
12. True
13. False—It was Billy Gilbert.
14. True
15. True
16. False
17. False—It was a remake of *Here Comes Mr. Jordan* (1941).
18. True
19. True
20. False—Donald O'Connor starred.

Romance-Melodrama

NAME THAT STAR!

1. Charles Boyer
2. Ingrid Bergman
3. Cary Grant
4. Irene Dunne
5. Joan Crawford
6. Joan Fontaine
7. Spencer Tracy
8. Bette Davis
9. Ronald Colman
10. Rex Harrison
11. Rock Hudson
12. Katharine Hepburn
13. Elizabeth Taylor
14. Ginger Rogers
15. Gregory Peck
16. Dorothy McGuire
17. William Holden
18. Ava Gardner
19. Lana Turner
20. Rita Hayworth

NAME THAT STAR! multiple choice

1. b	11. c	21. a	31. e
2. c	12. a	22. b	32. a
3. d	13. c	23. d	33. d
4. e	14. e	24. a	34. b
5. a	15. e	25. c	35. a
6. c	16. c	26. d	36. d
7. b	17. b	27. b	37. c
8. d	18. c	28. c	38. b
9. e	19. e	29. a	39. d
10. d	20. c	30. a	40. c

NAME THAT MOVIE!

1. An Affair to Remember *(1957)*
2. Magnificent Obsession *(1935)*
3. All This and Heaven Too *(1940)*
4. Ash Wednesday *(1973)*
5. Dear Heart *(1964)*
6. Green Dolphin Street *(1947)*
7. Desire under the Elms *(1958)*

8. Brief Encounter *(1945)*
9. Picnic *(1956)*
10. Autumn Leaves *(1956)*
11. The Blue Angel *(1930)*
12. Marty *(1955)*
13. Letter from an Unknown Woman *(1948)*
14. Sunset Boulevard *(1950)*

15. A Stolen Life *(1946)*
16. Intermezzo *(1939)*
17. Dark Victory *(1939)*
18. The Constant Nymph *(1943)*
19. Cyrano de Bergerac *(1950)*
20. Anna Karenina *(1935)*

TRUE OR FALSE?

1. False—Robert Redford starred.
2. True
3. False—Carroll Baker played Mama Harlow.
4. False—It's a family melodrama.
5. False—Harris played a miner who becomes a successful rugby player.
6. True
7. True
8. True
9. True
10. True
11. False—Sarah Miles played the female lead.

12. True
13. True
14. False—Laurence Harvey starred.
15. False—Debbie Reynolds starred as Tammy in 1957, though Sandra Dee played that role in the two film sequels.
16. True
17. True
18. True
19. True
20. False—Michael Caine co-starred with Elizabeth Taylor.

Epics

NAME THAT STAR!

1. Charlton Heston
2. Robert Taylor
3. Victor Mature
4. Richard Burton
5. Kirk Douglas
6. Yul Brynner
7. James Mason
8. Cedric Hardwicke
9. Anthony Quinn
10. Charles Laughton
11. Laurence Olivier
12. John Barrymore
13. Ralph Richardson
14. Orson Welles
15. Peter Ustinov
16. Vincent Price
17. Fredric March
18. John Carradine
19. Errol Flynn
20. George Sanders

NAME THAT STAR! multiple choice

1. b
2. a
3. c
4. d
5. a
6. a
7. d
8. a
9. a
10. d
11. a
12. b
13. e
14. c
15. d
16. a
17. d
18. b
19. b
20. a
21. c
22. b
23. c
24. b
25. c
26. a
27. d
28. b
29. c
30. b
31. c
32. d
33. e
34. c
35. b
36. a
37. a
38. d
39. c
40. b

NAME THAT MOVIE!

1. The Agony and the Ecstasy *(1965)*
2. Ben Hur *(1959)*
3. The Robe *(1953)*
4. The Towering Inferno *(1974)*
5. The Bible *(1966)*
6. The Vikings *(1958)*
7. Rembrandt *(1937)*
8. Helen of Troy *(1955)*
9. The Ten Commandments *(1956)*
10. Lust for Life *(1956)*
11. Alexander the Great *(1956)*
12. The Egyptian *(1954)*
13. El Cid *(1961)*

14. Moby Dick *(1956)*
15. Things to Come *(1936)*
16. One Million B.C. *(1939)*
17. The Rains Came *(1939)*
18. The Last Days of Pompeii *(1935)*
19. Caesar and Cleopatra *(1945)*
20. The Thief of Bagdad *(1940)*

TRUE OR FALSE?

1. True
2. True
3. True
4. True
5. True
6. True
7. True
8. False—Omar Sharif starred.
9. True
10. False—Olivier directed and starred in *Hamlet* (1948).
11. True
12. True
13. False—John Gielgud starred.
14. True
15. False—Peter O'Toole starred.
16. False—*Little Caesar* (1930) was a gangster film.
17. False—It was about the founding of a famous insurance company.
18. True
19. True
20. False—Paul Newman starred.

Science Fiction

NAME THAT STAR!

1. Beverly Garland
2. Jeff Morrow
3. Richard Carlson
4. Barbara Rush
5. Walter Pidgeon
6. Ray Milland
7. Charlton Heston
8. Rod Taylor
9. Barbara Shelley
10. John Agar
11. William Hopper
12. Michael Rennie
13. James Olson
14. Hugh Marlowe
15. Julie Christie
16. Vincent Price
17. Peter Cushing
18. John Emery
19. Richard Dreyfuss
20. Gene Barry

NAME THAT STAR! multiple choice

1. d
2. c
3. b
4. b
5. a
6. e
7. c
8. d
9. e
10. e
11. c
12. b
13. c
14. c
15. a
16. a
17. a
18. b
19. d
20. b
21. c
22. a
23. b
24. a
25. b
26. b
27. d
28. b
29. c
30. c
31. a
32. a
33. d
34. c
35. b
36. e
37. d
38. b
39. c
40. b

NAME THAT MOVIE!

1. Invasion of the Body Snatch-ers *(1956)*
2. Kronos *(1957)*
3. The Thing from Another World *(1951)*
4. The Andromeda Strain *(1970)*
5. The Day the Earth Stood Still *(1951)*
6. Invaders from Mars *(1953)*
7. Not of This Earth *(1957)*
8. Five Million Miles to Earth *or* Quatermass and the Pit, *Br.,* *(1967)*

9. Village of the Damned *(1960)*
10. 2001: A Space Odyssey *(1968)*
11. This Island Earth *(1955)*
12. Forbidden Planet *(1956)*
13. It Came from Outer Space *(1953)*
14. The War of the Worlds *(1952)*
15. Silent Running *(1971)*
16. Logan's Run *(1976)*
17. The Forbin Project *or* Colossus: The Forbin Project, *Br.,* *(1969)*
18. When Worlds Collide *(1951)*
19. Soylent Green *(1973)*
20. The Man in the White Suit *(1951)*

TRUE OR FALSE?

1. True
2. True
3. False—A diamond laser beam threatens the world.
4. True
5. False—Atomic explosions moved the Earth's orbit closer to the Sun.
6. False—A miniaturized sub travels through a man's bloodstream up into his brain.
7. True
8. True
9. True
10. True
11. True
12. False—A man out sailing is exposed to a strange radio- active mist and he begins to shrink in size.
13. True
14. False—There were four se- quels: *Beneath the Planet of the Apes* (1970), *Escape from the Planet of the Apes* (1971), *Conquest of the Planet of the Apes* (1972) and *Battle for the Planet of the Apes* (1973)
15. True
16. False—The Martians had only one eye.
17. False
18. True
19. True
20. True

War

NAME THAT STAR!

1. Dana Andrews
2. Humphrey Bogart
3. William Holden
4. Robert Mitchum
5. Henry Fonda
6. Errol Flynn
7. James Cagney
8. Robert Ryan
9. Gregory Peck
10. Randolph Scott
11. John Wayne
12. Richard Widmark
13. Walter Pidgeon
14. Burt Lancaster
15. James Mason
16. Kirk Douglas
17. Frank Sinatra
18. Frank Lovejoy
19. Van Johnson
20. Gary Cooper

NAME THAT STAR! multiple choice

1. b	11. c	21. b	31. b
2. c	12. e	22. a	32. e
3. a	13. c	23. b	33. a
4. c	14. d	24. d	34. b
5. a	15. c	25. e	35. a
6. b	16. b	26. e	36. b
7. d	17. c	27. a	37. a
8. d	18. b	28. e	38. d
9. e	19. b	29. c	39. c
10. d	20. c	30. a	40. d

NAME THAT MOVIE!

1. Lifeboat *(1944)*
2. The Longest Day *(1972)*
3. The Desert Fox *(1951)*
4. The Purple Heart *(1944)*
5. A Walk in the Sun *(1946)*
6. From Here to Eternity *(1953)*
7. The Battle of the Bulge *(1965)*
8. Thirty Seconds Over Tokyo *(1944)*
9. The Gallant Hours *(1959)*
10. Command Decision *(1949)*
11. In Harm's Way *(1965)*

12. The Blue Max *(1966)*
13. Sergeant York *(1941)*
14. Anzio *(1968)*
15. The Immortal Sergeant *(1943)*
16. Cast a Giant Shadow *(1966)*
17. Flying Tigers *(1942)*

18. Dr. Strangelove or: How I Stopped Worrying and Learned to Love the Bomb *(1963)*
19. The Dirty Dozen *(1967)*
20. Von Ryan's Express *(1965)*

TRUE OR FALSE?

1. True
2. True
3. True
4. False—Cliff Robertson starred.
5. False—Greer Garson starred.
6. True
7. False—Academy Award winning war films included: *All Quiet on the Western Front* (1930); *Mrs. Miniver* (1942); *The Best Years of Our Lives* (1946); *From Here to Eternity* (1953); *The Bridge on the River Kwai* (1957); *Lawrence of Arabia* (1962); Patton (1970).
8. True
9. False—Robinson appeared in *Destroyer* (1943), *Mr.*

Winkle Goes to War (1944) and *Journey Together* (1944).
10. True
11. True
12. True
13. False—John Payne *was* the star.
14. False—It was the story of an American pilot and a Japanese naval officer who were stranded together on a tiny island in the Pacific and starred Lee Marvin.
15. True
16. False—John Wayne co-starred.
17. True
18. True
19. True
20. True